REFLECTING MEN

SALLY CLINE
DALE SPENDER

REFLECTING MEN

AT TWICE THEIR
NATURAL SIZE

cartoons by Riana Duncan

ANDRE DEUTSCH

First published 1987 by
André Deutsch Limited
105-106 Great Russell Street London WC1B 3LJ

British Library Cataloguing in Publication Data

Cline, Sally
  Reflecting men at twice their natural size.
  1. Men 2. Women 3. Interpersonal relations
  I. Title II. Spender, Dale
  305.3 HQ1090

ISBN 0–233–97871–2

Phototypeset by Falcon Graphic Art Limited
Wallington, Surrey
Printed in Great Britain by
Ebenezer Baylis & Son Ltd, Worcester

Women have served all these centuries as looking-glasses, possessing the magic and delicious power of reflecting the figure of a man at twice its natural size.

Virginia Woolf, *A Room of One's Own*, 1928

ACKNOWLEDGEMENTS

Sally Cline

To ISABEL CLARE, ANTHEA HILLS, and my long-suffering close friend KATHY BOWLES who spent tedious hours transcribing and typing tortuous tapes, a big thank you.

To JANICE MCDONALD at the Cambridge University Library, who painstakingly tracked down lost references, great gratitude.

To AUDREY CECILIA JACKSON for inspired snippets of wisdom; to ANNE GURNETT for her untiring example as a devoted workaholic; to DIANA MUTIMER for her warmth and strength, real debts are owed.

To ADELE MCSORLEY, now safely away from the words in Canada, enormous appreciation for the years of support and tape-typing in England. KATHY MULLEN'S unfailing kindness and practical help, and CAROL JONES' unstinting availability as a listener and critic, are measures of our friendship.

VAL UNSWORTH'S shared understandings of the difficulties of trying to be both a mother and a writer, make her more than a good neighbour.

The constant support of the CAMBRIDGE A LEVEL SOCIOLOGY GROUP (LESLEY ANNAND, KAY THOMAS, MARILYN JONES, GAILE WALKER, DIANA BRAVERMAN) and the sturdy criticisms of the CAMBRIDGE WOMEN WRITERS' COLLECTIVE (JOY MAGEZIS, PAULINA PALMER, LINDA QUARRIE, JANE FRANCES, PAT GAVIGNET) and their help with the pilot study were invaluable.

PRUDENCE JONES, LESLEY HOLLY, BREKKE LARSEN, FOSSIL, and most of all MICHELLE STANWORTH interrupted busy lives to offer stimulating suggestions and mull over ideas.

CANDIDA LACEY'S gimlet eyes and ESTHER WHITBY'S never-ending patience made them concerned as well as correcting editors.

My writing could not have taken place without the contribution of three households:

1) At Sennen Cove, Cornwall, I was constantly ferried in JEAN ADAM'S and RON WARNER'S cars; chapters were composed on BARBARA WARNER'S elderly amazing typewriter; and shared laughter and a room of my own provided by JEAN in her idyllic Sunset Heights, no better place for creation.

2) At Cambridge, SUE generously gave up her study and exchanged exciting thoughts, MANDY made coffee, listened to the words, and sorted out the moans, BABY ADAM and my goddaughter CHARLOTTE gave essential encouraging hugs; and KATE and SARAH daily allowed invasion into their peaceful home, SARAH to offer me space, and KATE something deeper than mere academic understandings.

3) At Garden Walk, Cambridge, my home, throughout the final draft MEGAN WILBY interrupted her dissertation to read, criticise and enthuse; and throughout every draft MARM and CAS and VIC and BEC switched off their stereos and switched on their attention. CAS willingly photocopied and provided paper and support; BEC lent her taperecorder and her gentle concentration; VIC was a perpetual bubble of interested involvement and zany ideas; and MARMOSET spent hours in Tattie's Restaurant subduing her own needs and her A Level problems to listen to the horrors of the Mother's manuscript. BA SHEPPARD'S years of faith enabled me to write and stopped me from losing my way. For her passionate emotional support and fierce intellectual detachment, and for her sense of humour, there are no adequate words of thanks. Just as well, she has had enough of words! I dedicate this book to her.

The last stages of the book would have been untenable without WENDY MULFORD'S care. She was never too involved with her own writing and repairs to shut herself off from me and mine. Thank you for opening up the possibilities, Wendy.

All stages of the book would have been unworkable without my partner DALE'S months of elasticated tolerance and years of affectionate understanding. I have stretched both to the limit, and I am glad that I had the chance.

I would also like to thank two men who have helped me very much: my doctor, Bernard Reiss, and my bank manager, Mr C. J. Fryer.

Dale Spender

I would like to thank the many women who talked with us and who helped to make this book possible; I would also like to thank GLYNIS WOOD who transformed many bits and pieces of copy into a clean manuscript and helped to make this book possible. And to CANDIDA ANN LACEY, who edited the manuscript, who skilfully brought together the authors' contributions and various views, many thanks must go for achieving what some might have seen as the impossible.

I would also like to thank SALLY CLINE for her wit, warmth and writing; it has been a pleasure working with her.

CONTENTS

INTRODUCTION

Men have egos; women do not. This is a sex difference and deserves attention. So it is surprising to find that outside the popular literature of women's magazines – which advises women on how to manage men's egos – little serious information about this male organ is available.

Even more surprising, however, is the absence of serious discussion about this amongst women. Despite more than a decade of feminist deliberations there has been no debate on the male ego; not on its origin, its nature, nor its effects on women. Such silence calls for an explanation. Clearly the male ego exists; it is not simply the creation of women's magazines. Women know a good deal about men's egos even though they seldom talk about them in private, less in public and almost never in the presence of men.

What a male ego is, where it comes from, how it works – and why? – are the major issues of this book. One reason for raising them is that they have not been addressed seriously as contemporary issues before. Apart from a book by Beata Bishop in 1977, entitled *Below the Belt: An Irreverent Analysis of the Male Ego*, we can find no sustained discussion or description of this phenomenon. And although it has not been our intention actually to undertake a 'reverent' analysis of the male ego, we have sought to be serious in our perusal of this male propensity, partly because we are convinced that it pervades women's lives.

Our research, which began innocently enough, did not take the form in which we now present it. It started with our random observations on the way women look after the feelings of men. We looked at other women – we monitored ourselves – and we could not help wondering why women were so concerned to 'protect' and to please men. Once questions like this were raised they would not go away. They tugged at the corners of our busy lives and demanded our attention. They made their presence felt as we dealt with our daily world and came to understand that in an ordinary day we were doing our best to promote goodwill among men.

Sitting in a restaurant one night, we realised that it was no longer possible for us to put aside these issues we had raised conversationally. We turned our attention from the menu and listed what we already knew. We knew, for example, that we had no evidence that this protective behaviour of women towards men was reciprocated. While each of us had experienced kindness, concern, generosity from individual men, we were completely convinced that as a class, men were not concerned with cosseting the emotions and feelings of women. We put this, our first point, to the test.

A random sampling of our fellow diners (central London; pasta; medium price range) supported this conviction. We asked them whether women 'managed' the emotions of men and both sexes confirmed that this was the general rule. But when we asked whether it worked in reverse, whether men managed the emotions of women, many of the women began to laugh; others, and some of the men, told us that the question was ridiculous.

One woman summed up the situation: 'What you're really asking about is the *male* ego,' she informed us, 'and of course people are going to laugh and say you're ridiculous if you try to turn it round. There isn't a *female* ego, you know. It's a contradiction in terms!'

This was really the foundation stone. Not only did her comments help support our stance, they clarified some of the issues as well. For in this 'pilot study' we found that it was widely believed that managing emotions was something that women did for men. Neither women nor men believed that the favour was returned, partly because the idea that women might have egos was not generally entertained.

At the top of our list, we had the heading '*male* egos'. This was followed by 'the way women manage them' and, thus, our list of women's work steadily grew. Some of the entries we made in that restaurant, where this book really began, retained their place as common examples of the ways in which women handle men's feelings.

Looking around the tables, we were struck by just how many women were smiling at men and how few men were smiling in return. Women were smiling at the men they were with: at the

"I HAD AN EGO ONCE BUT I GAVE IT UP WHEN I GOT MARRIED."

waiters; on her way across the room, one woman even smiled at a man who not only was clearly a stranger but whose sudden surge from his chair dramatically impeded her progress. She apologised (we eavesdropped) and smiled, assuring him that all was well. Whilst his feelings were obviously considered, little effort, from what we could see and hear, was being made to care for hers. Even had she been physically hurt, we suspected that she would have concealed the injury in order to save the clumsy man from further embarrassment.

We continued to observe and to listen, to note and to speculate; we had a data-gathering field day in that restaurant.

We watched two women who appeared to be quite content chatting to each other. They were approached by a man who interrupted their conversation. And they smiled. After a few 'polite' exchanges, he withdrew. We allowed a decent interval to pass before apologising for our intrusion and introducing ourselves. We asked the women whether they would mind giving us the details of the incident which we had been unable to hear.

Yes, they told us, the man who had come to their table had been a stranger. No, they had never seen him before. They hadn't noticed him and his friend. No, they had not invited him, nor, to their knowledge, had they attracted his attention. He had come to request the pleasure of their company and it had been rather awkward getting him to take no for an answer.

What exactly did he say, we asked, trying to establish why the women had smiled at the man. While it could have been a source of amusement that he had said, 'As you two are alone, why don't you join my friend and me,' we realised that the women did not see anything funny in a man describing them as being 'alone'. There was nothing in what he had *said* that warranted a smile as far as they were concerned.

'We didn't want to join him and his friend,' she explained. 'But we didn't want him to feel badly about it. I don't think he felt rejected.'

Here, in one exchange in a London restaurant, we encountered some of the problems and practices that were to emerge as the fundamental issues in our project. We watched (and monitored ourselves) and noted how frequently a woman would come to the rescue of a man who was being embarrassing, rude or stupid. We watched women protecting men, placating men, propping up men's pride and generally managing the emotional environment so that the feelings of men were mellowed and manipulated.

On more than one occasion, we saw two women winking at each other as together they soothed a man's ruffled feathers. While there was no 'conversation' between such women, there was no doubt that there was some communication about what they were doing.

We wrote up countless examples of the way women worked to make men feel good. We noted how women made men feel wanted and needed. We listed all the ploys we could find that women used to place men at the centre of attention and to reassure them of their significance.

And we began to ask why.

Why should women make such a sustained effort to boost the egos of men? Why is it so important to women to ensure that men suffer no loss of face? Why is there so little discussion of this peculiarly female activity? What part are women playing in perpetuating the primacy of men by putting so much effort into making men look good and feel good?

Was this something to do with women or something to do with men? Were men such emotionally fragile creatures that they couldn't get through life without the constant care and consideration of women? Did they have to be flattered into thinking they were first and foremost, in order to deal with the world? Or was it that women wanted the supremacy of men?

These were difficult questions and they led us to some disconcerting explanations. And the only way we could check and clarify them was to turn to women, and to ask them why they behaved in this way.

But how to go about it? What to ask? What to say? We realised that we were going to require women to reveal some of the most intimate details of their lives and we suspected that, as there was so little discussion on this aspect of the relationship between the sexes, the topic was taboo. We could find articles in women's magazines which assured us that the male ego was alive – and that it was the task of women to keep it well – but the concept of the male ego was only part of the problem that we wanted to investigate. We began to look to the past rather than the present for an elaboration of the 'problem' we wanted to pursue. While we could find no mention of women's emotional management of men in current research literature or philosophical treatises, we were convinced that this behaviour was not new. We suspected that women had been relating to men in this way for centuries; we wondered whether the problem had been analysed before.

It was Virginia Woolf who gave us our focus. Tucked away among the gems of wisdom in her discussion of women's self realisation in *A Room of One's Own* – written in 1928 – there is a paragraph which not only confirmed the existence of the problem but also succinctly summarised and labelled it:

5

> Women have served all these centuries as looking-glasses
> possessing the magic and delicious power of reflecting the
> figure of man at twice its natural size (p. 35).

And her question was – as ours had been – why? Why did women
possess this *power*? Not only did she ask why women magnified
the figure of man, she also asked what happened when they
stopped.

On the surface her explanation is self-evident; for if women
cease to reflect men at twice their natural size, she says, the result
is perfectly predictable. If a woman 'begins to tell the truth, the
figure in the looking-glass shrinks, his fitness for life is
diminished' (p. 36).

And this, too, is part of our project and our book. With the
words of Virginia Woolf inscribed in our minds, we set out to ask
not just why women reflect men, but what happens when they
stop.

The first and most surprising thing that we found was that
there was not one woman to whom we had to explain what we
meant by *reflecting men*. The topic may be under-elaborated and
un-encoded but the reality of it is certainly not unknown to
women. During the course of our interviews we saw that all
women reflect men; that they do so for different reasons and with
different results. We found, moreover, that this is the basis of the
relationship between the sexes.

1

CONFESSIONS

Before we set out to interview women on the whys and where-fores of reflecting men, we decided that a little introspection would not go astray; what did *we* do to reflect men? And why did we do it? If we were going to make judgements about this behaviour, perhaps it would be a good idea to begin with some judgements about ourselves. We realised that we already knew a great deal about the process: what we hadn't looked at in any detail were the reasons. We conducted our first 'interviews' with each other. And we began with our own profiles on what we do – and why we do it – when it comes to the management of the emotions of men.

Dale Spender

My starting point was that in my earlier research on mixed-sex conversations I had come to appreciate that men talked more than women. I had been able to document the greater number of interruptions performed by men (approximately 99%) and the greater extent to which men determined the conversation topics. I had also found that 'What you mean is . . .' is one of the most common utterances of men (on my tapes) as they talk to women. And while I had used this research it began to assume a new significance in the context of reflecting men. For I realised that when women were interrupted by men (sometimes rudely), when they had the topic of conversation taken from them (often with the 'take over' of 'what you mean is') they rarely protested. On the contrary, when I replayed those tapes I could sometimes *hear* the smile of the woman who made way for the man to take the conversational floor. There are many 'How very interesting' and 'What did you do then?' and 'I'm most impressed . . . do go on' comments made by women on the tapes. And each time I listen to those supportive and eliciting comments coming from the women . . . it is my own voice that I can hear.

This is not surprising. It could just as easily be me preparing the conversational space for men. I too have indulged in this form of verbal behaviour with the opposite sex – at least since adolescence. I would like to present myself as the strong independent feminist who has never gone to such accommodating lengths, but to do so would be to deceive.

On social occasions, at work, talking to publishers and reviewers, I must admit that I still engage in the 'And what did *you* do then' pattern which is familiar to women even if it goes unnoticed by men. And I know why I do it. I do it to survive, economically and emotionally. While it is unlikely that the publisher and the reviewer (on whom my livelihood depends) are going to be favourably disposed towards a 'rude' and abrasive author, economics isn't the only reason for my polite and pleasant disposition towards 'the boss'. There is also an element of wanting to be approved of, to be liked, which influences my behaviour; it is this which is more difficult to admit to and to understand.

For I think there is a limit – or I know there is for me – to the number of times that I can withstand full-scale social censure. I cannot fight every instance of sexism and I cannot cope with constant 'rejection', with the result that I conform to the social code, the code of caring for men's emotions, except when I specifically choose to take a stand. So I continue to say 'Oh really? Goodness me, how very interesting!' and to encourage men to feel at ease, to feel that they are in good hands and to help them to talk . . . most of the time. I continue to reassure many men of my interest when I verge on being bored to tears.

On more than one occasion I have included myself in my own research, and I have found that I behave in exactly the same way as other women do. I help men to talk, to feel good, at ease, expansive, to be verbally dominant, even when the express purpose of my involvement has been to obtain a fair share of the conversation time. Again and again my tapes have recorded the evidence to be used against me; again and again they have revealed that in conversation with men it is almost unknown for any woman to talk for more than one third of the time.* This is in itself quite astonishing; what is more astonishing, however, is that women consistently report that they had a fair share of the conversation, even if their 'share' was less than 20%.

When I first began to amass these findings, they represented something of a challenge to me. I set up conversations with men (which were taped) and I determined to talk for 50% of the time. Even when the disapproval started, I persevered. I have believed myself to be aggressive, rude, inconsiderate, domineering and unpleasant, as I have tried to get an equal share. And before the tapes were analysed I was prepared to claim that it felt as though I *had* talked for 50% of the time; perhaps I had even talked for longer? This was certainly the opinion of my male conversationalists; without exception each volunteered the information that I was impossible, that I didn't listen to a word he said, and that I was overbearingly rude.

Yet never had I talked for more than 42% of the time. My average for such 'unacceptable' behaviour is 39%. Which says something about the amount of verbal space that both sexes consider a proper share for women and men. While women encourage men to speak (and there are some who need little encouragement) for about two thirds of the time, the social code is observed. But let women take more than one third, and there is a social disaster. One does not need to be a mathematician to deduce that only while men are receiving twice the entitlement of women, does the conversation proceed smoothly. The bitter pill for me to swallow, however, is that even when I don't want to, I too behave in this way.

I am fully aware of how the system works, but knowledge, it seems, does not make one immune; it does not always lead to refusal to comply. I cannot quite decide whether it is because I cannot unlearn what I was so assiduously taught, or whether it is because I cannot bear the brunt of outright disapproval which prevents me from *taking* my equal share of the conversation, and which prompts me to make all those solicitous noises. Neither explanation is particularly flattering.

There was a time when I wondered whether this form of

---

* There are some exceptions. When the woman is a medical practitioner, solicitor, educator – or in some other profession and informal professional advice is being sought, women can talk for more than 33% of the time. And Mrs Thatcher is another exception.

behaviour was culturally specific. That was before I spent a few weeks in Sweden, where I could not understand a single word. I didn't need to. Sitting one night in a restaurant I was able to observe much the same behaviour that had prompted this project as I saw couple after couple come in; the behaviour of the woman – and the man – was invariably the same. No matter how tall she was, the woman always managed to seat herself lower than the man, with the result that she could look up to him. I would hear that eliciting tone – those encouraging sounds – as she tempted him to talk. I would watch her sit forward, drawing him out and then withdrawing into her seat once he was in full flight. And his expansion was not just verbal; I watched him take two thirds of the table space and the leg room. And then I knew that this female habit was not peculiar to the English, nor to English-speaking countries.

When I have tried to 'teach' this topic, I have generally encountered some fierce resistance, from women as well as men. It is as if there is a fear that *all* will come tumbling down if the cover is blown. I once tried to teach to some postgraduate students that body posture (looking up to him), and smiling, are part of the elaborate ritual of reflection. I pointed out that women were expected to smile at men, to indicate that they were noticed, that women were pleased to see them. If women did not fulfil this role, there was trouble. I used as evidence the smile boy-cott of the New York receptionists (first proposed as a strategy in 1970 by Shulamith Firestone). For one week the receptionists refused to smile. And there was one disaster after another. It was not just the immediate, and interminable, queries of 'What's wrong with you?' although these responses were significant enough, and difficult to handle. Some men got abusive – wildly so. Receptionists were accused of 'ruining the day' of many a man, of deliberate 'sabotage', and cases of physical threat were not uncommon.

My students questioned the validity of this research (which has not been written up in a respectable academic journal), so I suggested we conduct our own experiment. Accordingly, three unsmiling women students set off to run the gauntlet of a short pathway, and their fellow students (who were observing) were astonished. All three women were accosted; 'What's wrong with you?' was the standard demand. One was told 'Cheer up, love; it's not that bad', and the same woman was twice physically stopped and abused. Because they were unsmiling. Because they did not indicate they were pleased to see a man.

After that, I had no need to reassert that women are expected to smile for men, even expected to smile at total strangers. I did, however, need to explain: to them – why it happens; to myself – why I still do it.

It was Florence Nightingale who wrote that men are 'irritated with women for not being happy. They take it as a personal offence' (in Ray Strachey, 1928 p.396). A man is meant to be the centre of a woman's existence. She should be miserable in his absence and shine in his presence. She must be cheerful – smiling – when he is around. It is an expression of her gratitude and of his importance. This is why he can 'take it as a personal offence' if she does not glow when he appears on the scene. Florence Nightingale knew what was happening; what she did not know was that the practice would be so hard to eradicate.

'No man wants to come home to an unhappy woman.' I was the recipient of this well-meaning advice for many years. It was during my pre-feminist days when I burnt with resentment about the double standard that applied to marriage and work. Why did I have two jobs when he had only one? Why should I be shopping, cooking, cleaning when he was watching sport on television? I made a lot of noise about the injustice of these arrangements and I was continually warned about the error of my ways: I was becoming embittered, I was informed. If I didn't improve – if I didn't stop nagging and start being appreciative – I might soon find myself in a much worse position. At least when he was watching television he was at home, and in *my* company.

But he wouldn't stay at home if I kept protesting and sulking. It was my job to make home a pleasant place. To make him feel wanted. To be pleased to see him. And whenever I retorted, 'Half his luck! I wish someone would go to the same trouble to make home such a pleasant place for me!' I was rebuked. How selfish and hard could I be?

In my experience it is not uncommon to find men saying that they don't like to see women doing domestic chores. It makes them feel uneasy – particularly if they are sitting reading the paper at the time. Perhaps this is one 'achievement' of the modern women's movement. Men have come so far as to understand that it is not really fair that women should have the complete responsibility for domestic chores. This is why they are uncomfortable when it is the case that *both* have done a hard day's work, and afterwards she is still buzzing round the kitchen or racing through the ironing, while he is relaxing. She makes him feel guilty. He may end his unease by insisting that she come and sit down, that she relax, leave the dishes till the morning, and let the ironing go. But she knows it won't go away. To preserve the peace she may try to get through it all while he is not around. This is one reason she gets to bed later and gets up earlier. It's why I did.

I am sure I am not the only woman who has come to appreciate the desirability – even necessity – of being home first and of making sure that all is in order – for him. I am not the only woman who has put my own interests and activities aside and catered exclusively for his upon his entry. And I wasn't economically dependent on the man for whom I did all this.

But 'women have no means given them whereby they can resist these claims' for attention and centrality that are made upon them by men, Florence Nightingale wrote knowingly last century. 'They are taught from their infancy upwards that it is wrong, ill-tempered, and a misunderstanding of women's mission (with a great M) if they do not allow themselves *willingly* to be interrupted at all hours' (ibid., p.403). It is part of the relationship between the sexes that women should willingly – and cheerfully – allow themselves to be interrupted by men: at the work place; at home; in conversation. 'Of course it's not too much trouble . . .' as they put aside what they are doing and give their undivided attention to the men. This is why women smile – rather than scowl – when interrupted by men. It is the mark of being a proper woman and of making a man feel important.

For more than four years I was involved in my research to establish that men talked more than women. After I had completed my report (for the daily research still continues), I experienced some satisfaction at the thought that I had helped to challenge the conventional wisdom that it was women who were the talkative sex. Then I found an account of the first women's rights conference in the United States. It was held in Salem, Ohio, in 1850 and it had one peculiar characteristic. It was officered entirely by women; not a man was allowed to sit on the platform, to speak, to vote. 'NEVER DID MEN SUFFER SO,' wrote Elizabeth Cady Stanton who had played a part in setting up this peculiar arrangement. 'They implored just to say a word; but no – the President was inflexible – no man should be heard. If one meekly arose to make a suggestion he was at once ruled out of order. For the first time in the world's history, men learned how to sit in silence when questions they were interested in were under discussion' (Stanton *et al*, 1881, vol I, p.110, original emphasis).

Some of the men were enraged by this treatment. How could women expect to present a convincing case if they treated men in this barbarous fashion? Neither then nor now have men taken kindly to being silenced in the presence of women. But apart from seeing my own satisfaction sliding away when I realised that Elizabeth Cady Stanton had come to the same conclusions as I had – 130 years before and without benefit of a research degree – I realised that her 'strategy' had potential.

Whenever I tried to discuss these research findings, however, I met with many protests. 'Your material might be all right but your manner lets you down. It's too threatening. You have an accusing tone,' I was told. On one occasion I was speaking at a conference and was listing my findings – that males talk more, interrupt more, and are more likely to insist on telling you what is *really* meant. Before I could finish I was interrupted by two men in the audience.

This was not true, they protested. It wasn't at all the way I described it. Men did not talk more, interrupt more, or insist that they knew all the answers. They would tell me what it was really like – and they proceeded to do so at great length. They were angry and emotional as they repudiated my aggressive, embittered and negative image of men. I presented my research findings – and they accused me of being a man-hater. It was clear that my facts were violating the social laws.

Later I was congratulated on setting up such a good example of male behaviour to illustrate my thesis. I didn't know whether it was an admission of success or failure to say I had nothing to do with it, that it hadn't been staged. But I kept thinking about those words of Elizabeth Cady Stanton.

Some men were extremely helpful. On the subject of education, for example, they readily acknowledged the validity of my research findings and deplored the way boys would be boys and take up all the verbal, physical and psychological space in social contexts and in classrooms. It was a disgrace, they said, that boys should spend so much time talking. What was needed in education was for boys to listen. Teachers should just start spending more time with the boys and instruct them in listening.

I was astonished. I had never realised just how *self*-centred men's solutions could be. Here was I documenting a problem, showing just how unfair it was that boys should monopolise so much of the teachers' time. And here were they agreeing – and suggesting as a solution – that teachers should spend *even more time* with the boys. Was there no way to break the habit of males' seeing themselves as central, and the needs of females as irrelevant?

Past and present, women have been expressing their gratitude to men who have behaved reasonably. Whenever a man has elected *not* to use his unfair advantages against women, he has been applauded. 'I've got a good husband – he'd never beat me.' 'My guy's wonderful – he lets me have my own life.' 'I'm lucky – my husband helps me with the housework.' These comments are not rare; they are the common currency of women's lives. And what does it mean when women give men prizes for behaving in a decent, responsible and reasonable fashion? What does it mean when women are grateful that their men are not tyrants?

Daily, almost hourly, women's efforts and achievements go unacknowledged while those of men are held up for all the world to admire. A mother may insist that she makes no distinctions between daughter and son, a teacher may be adamant that both sexes are treated the same; put it to the test, with one short tape recording and some elementary analysis, and we find boys being praised and girls being ignored. The reason we remain unaware is that this practice is so deeply entrenched in our value system that we simply accept it as part of the way the world works.

I have come to call it 'the rule of no more than one third'. Much of my research has been based on demonstrating that women get less than one third of so many resources . . . and that this is considered fair. Women get less than one third of the talk time, less than one third of teachers' attention; any more and women are seen to be getting too much. They are even seen to be dominating.

Only recently, I undertook some research on reviews of women's books. Women were getting 'more than their share' of review space, I was informed. To me, this sounded like another version of women as the talkative sex. So for six months I diligently measured the column inches of review space devoted to women's books in some major newspapers and literary period-icals. And at the end I was able to state – categorically and irrefutably – that women receive less than 6% of the column inches. Less than 6%, but to many it seems as though women are getting more than their share. Which gives you some idea of what women's share is supposed to be.

6% for women means 6% less for men. Is it really the case that such a small space for women takes away so much from men? Is it that men want to be the *only* sex to have the limelight? That any woman who is visible deprives them of their due?

Certainly it seems that the injunction that women should be passive has had the effect of ensuring that men are seen as active. So a woman who gains attention, who holds the floor, who gets reviewed, is seen as an intruder and can be accused of being aggressive.

Mrs Thatcher is a good example. Women who speak – and the rare women who speak with authority – are aggressive intruders. They are not reflecting men but standing in the spotlight themselves. They are seen as overbearing and bossy. Mrs Thatcher is accused of *not listening*. Research, I suspect, would show that Mrs Thatcher listens no more and no less than any other prime minister has done. But Mrs Thatcher is a woman. And she is not being measured against former prime ministers – but against the standard set for women.

Research, I suspect, would also reveal that Mrs Thatcher behaves to the men around her in much the same way as previous prime ministers have done. It is not the duty of the prime minister to reflect the men of the cabinet at twice their normal size. But Mrs Thatcher is not just the Prime Minister, she is a woman prime minister, and when she speaks authoritatively to her colleagues it is as a woman and not as a prime minister that she is judged. She is dominating – bossy – aggressive. Because *she* does not smile when she is interrupted. And so she offends.

I have no wish to hold up Mrs Thatcher as a model. But I cannot endorse a double standard. If it is necessary for prime ministers to listen – then all prime ministers should listen. There should be no penalty for a woman who behaves like a man when the behaviour of men is not a matter for reproach.

I would prefer to see male politicians emulating the positive aspects of women's behaviour: better that men should learn to act like women, than the reverse. For it is not the polite, careful, enhancing attitude of women that I am against: it is that they are obliged to adopt this manner without being treated politely, carefully, and enhancingly in return. Were men to acquire some of the skills that women have developed, skills of listening and managing, which make people feel good, there could be no cause for complaint. But it is only women who are required to behave in this way: it is only women who must be pleasant and polite, regardless. And it is the regardless that is difficult and demeaning.

When I look over my own life and see how often I flatter men, I know it is not just because I am cowardly. I know I have a commitment – no matter how corny it sounds – to the world being a pleasant place for all. And I know why I am reluctant to resort to reprimands and rebukes. So I smile when I am interrupted by a man. I do not contradict the man who tells me he is god's gift to women or the goddess's gift to the women's movement. I choose to leave him in a good mood, rather than a bad mood. As my sister says, it's a big job to change the world. You can't do it in five minutes. And when five minutes is all I've got, I keep things pleasant.

Theoretically I know that being polite and acquiescent has not had much of a success rate. Women tried for decades to be polite and to persuade men to give them the vote. It didn't work. But I cannot completely abandon my hopes of a more pleasant world for all. So I regularly do my maintenance bit. Like most women, I help men to feel good and hope that it pays some dividends. But I do not know if the end justifies the means.

Sally Cline

I look again at the brief. We do not want to circumscribe the possibilities open to contributors. So many possibilities over those last years. So many spoilt possibilities. So many years spent reflecting men. Some professionally and paid. Some privately and unpaid.

Publicly, for the first ten years of my working life, I made my living reflecting men and male values, as a journalist working for many of the male-dominated national newspapers in Fleet Street. In those days, the early sixties, it was considered a good career for a young woman straight out of university. I left college after graduating on a Friday and was lucky enough to land the job of every reporter's dreams on the Monday. My dreams were not, as now, of uncovering women's truths, of enlarging the possibilities of more truths around us, of taking risks on behalf of those of us largely excluded from power, resources, knowledge and honour. My hopes as a young 'girl reporter' were not even Gloria Steinem's 'daily rebellions or dreams of equality'. My fantasies were eminently prosaic. I was considered bright, knew myself to be ambitious, from the start I was intent on 'making it' in a man's world. I worked hard and conscientiously for several newspapers ranging from the *Observer* to the *Daily Mirror*. I wrote TV reviews, gossip stories for diary columns (somewhat hindered in my observations by extremely short sight and too much vanity to wear specs), occasional features about the subtly clever women behind the great men and frequent features about great men themselves. I tried to be objective, to be political, to be taken seriously. This meant I could not write about women or women's concerns; they were not matters either for objectivity or serious appraisal. Conservatively, I followed media stereotypes of masculinity and femininity. If the women I interviewed broke the pattern, secretly I admired them, and in print I lightly mocked them. Once I was fortunate enough to interview Françoise Gilot, Picasso's mistress, an amazing woman. I remember quietly thinking how lucky it was that the great master was dead or I'd never have got to talk to her at all. Each of my editors assured me that I wrote with what they termed 'sparkle'. This meant I was shallow, predictable and harmless. Moreover, I was seduced by seeing my words and my name in print. Then, as now, I knew that language has power. Then, as now, I recognised that language can be used as a means of changing reality, but as a journalist I rarely tried to use it in that way. On the occasions when I did, my copy would be spiked and my column would simply not appear. I was a fast learner and soon learnt to use the media language of male reflection; a language that too aptly serves the status quo.

I learnt to use it competently in order to belittle and betray blacks and homosexuals (these usually by omission), the working classes (these through stereotyping) and women (systematically through all available means). Gloria Steinem, also once a 'girl reporter', says that for her the worst experience was her own capitulation to the small humiliations and her own refusal to trust an emotional understanding of what was going on or even to trust her own experience. That statement fits my own memories exactly. There were many instances of this. Most of my trusted friends were women. Thankfully, I have always had loyal and intimate relationships with women and yet, publicly, I would accept the dictum that women were competitive, rivals for men and unable to get along with one another.

Adrienne Rich (1979) believes it is our duty to 'question everything'. But I hardly ever questioned anything. I never questioned the importance of 'news value' assignments like interviewing Helen Gurley Brown on the subject of men, or interviewing trendy men-about-town on the subject of leap year. Nor did I examine the shallow content that filled the trivial 'World of Sally Cline'.

The World of SALLY CLINE

TODAY I intend to kill a myth.

That old gem about diamonds. I know the demand has just overrun the supply. I know 400 million dollars' worth were bought in America alone last year.

I know that over 40 million American women are wearing them.

But they are NOT a girl's best friend.

At least not the girls I know. If they were, then you and I would be pretty friendless.

A spot check among women revealed that a girl's Best Friend is her:

Girdle
Money

Eyeliner
Money
Hairdresser
Best friend (moneyed)
Any man who tells her a lie about her face when she needs it.
Any man . . . when she needs him.
Any man who tells her the truth about her face when she needs it.

My poll

WHAT are my chances of being murdered? That, I read, is the big question women are asking today.

Is it? A snap survey centred on my own circle of questioning women and listening men proved otherwise.

These were the really big queries for women:

"Do you really think it suits me?"

"Are we going to wait until the final notice comes in before paying?"

"Who's going to be there?" Usually followed by: "Is he married?" And my own favourites:

"If I go to the hairdresser

at 10.30 tomorrow, could you be an angel and park the baby at the nursery, drop in the laundrette, see that the car gets a quick wash, but make sure you're back in time to pick me up before Claire's husband comes to collect her?"

How do you get the most out of a man? A finishing school has opened in East Berlin to teach attractive girls how to wheedle information from unsuspecting West German males.

They are trained to use narcotics, hypnosis, and even handle 6.35 mm automatics.

This may be the way Berlin babes hot up the cold war, but back in Britain even the stupidest spy knows you can't get a man with a gun.

It just isn't the way girls make friends and influence people.

Stand by, spies. Here's the Cline School of Persuasion.

Lesson one. Attract him.

Drop that gun. Use the weapon of inconsistency, Act unattainable. Don't laugh at his funny lines. Act accessible.

Laugh madly at his funny lines.

Lesson two. Distract him.

Drop drugs. Lure with allure. If a girl's after HIS mind make him think he's after HER body.

Lesson three. Put him under contract.

If you want him to talk, there's nothing quite so hypnotic as that old, old line: "Tell me about yourself darling."

I guarantee the Cline Code isn't a question of once you have caught him never let him go but once he's been found you'll have to send him to East Berlin to lose him.

I never questioned the social place I held as the brightest youngest girl reporter amongst a crowd of older, smarter, more talented men. I never even questioned the meaning of a word like 'talent'. And yet I did not have defective chromosomes. I had been well educated, held a good degree and felt at least as intelligent as most of the men in the newsrooms I worked in. Yet for eight years I continued to accept plausible male myths that contradicted and denied the experience of my own life and the life of every woman I knew well. Myths about motherhood. Myths about abortions. Myths about male violence. Perhaps the piece I am most bitterly ashamed of is the one about violence: I adopted the shocking and frivolous stance that many women were addicted to violence and therefore deserved it. I also consciously helped to perpetrate male myths about fashion, frippery, femininity and sexuality.

Despite these awful exposures, I still believe that I was not a frivolous young woman (I certainly knew that appearances were not everything) but I have to admit that I was proud, rather than ashamed, when I was made woman's editor of the *Daily Sketch*; the youngest woman's editor on Fleet Street, in charge of fashion, beauty and feminine interests for a paper so right wing its editor had been photographed in his Mosley-style blackshirt. My daily woman's page was aptly captioned SALLY CLINE'S PAGE: THE WOMAN'S PAGE *THAT MEN READ TOO*. (Occasionally it was headlined LADIES . . . AND GENTLEMEN . . . if the gentlemen care to be in the know.)

WHEN <u>HE</u> GETS INTO 'A STATE'

THIS is an end-of-page invitation to share with others a bit of what you've learned from life.

What do YOU do when your husband "gets into a state" about something? The symptoms are obvious. Something has "gone wrong at the office," the big row, the crises he brings home in a big, big way.

Mrs. Charles Mcnamara, wife of America's Defence Chief (a job, if ever there was one, where the crises never stop), has just been giving her advice. It's simple:

As Mr. M expounds the frightful fortunes of the day, Mrs. M lets her indignation surpass even his – and nearly always (she says) it works.

Her own torrent of protest against such savage injustice has the effect of lessening his own – and leading him to keep the crisis in calmer compass!

What's your technique? On a postcard, please. Addressed to: "Crisis," Daily Sketch, Carmelite Street, London, E.C.4. Ten guineas for the best postcard received by Friday of this week...

Many of my pages were devoted to men and their interests:

What <u>YOU MAY WELL ASK</u> are MEN doing on the Women's Page?

AS far as most girls go – men, drat 'em, are a necessity. And this page cannot ignore them forever.

Today . . . pushed by Queen magazine, which has already put out a male supplement, Woman's Journal, which launches Men's Journal in its next issue, Vogue, which brings out Men in Vogue in November, and male fashion king Pierre Cardin, who last week told me: "It is men's fashion that is undergoing revolution, not women's" . . . this page has succumbed.

which went on to discuss men's fashion.

Why shouldn't men read it? All sparkle and no threat. Line after line of reflecting men. Line after line of dividing women. Dividing them from each other. Dividing each from herself. In the office and on flights abroad to expense-account places like Singapore or New York, I glowed with delight when men told me they couldn't talk to their wives/mistresses/secretaries, but they could talk to me. I recall even laughing at the office dirty jokes and put-downs about other women, and feeling glad I was different. It never occurred to me that I might be letting my sisters down. In the sixties I had no sisters – at least, not publicly.

I wrote for women readers, but the men who owned my words told me I was not like them so I did not have to try to find a language to identify with them. Today, I know it is better to stay silent than to speak in the tongue that flatters and lies, and ultimately connives with the enemy. In the sixties, I spent patient hardworking hours of my time writing words that wittily devalued women's experiences, that cleverly destroyed women's identity. I used the language of male reflection to write a daily sparkling assent to all women's diminution.

Tillie Olsen (1978) talks of 'unnatural silences' (p.21) which are imposed by the demands of men (and children) upon the hours and lives of women. These unnatural silences became for many years my private understandings. But I believe there are also unnatural speeches. Those words and phrases which are imposed by the demands of men upon the lips and lives of women. Those speeches which reflected all men larger than life and diminished all women to deathly shadows. *These unnatural speeches became my public understandings.*

Looking back on my early life as a journalist I now realise that I did not choose Reflecting Men as a subject to write about in the eighties. It had already chosen me years ago.

Today when my right-on feminist friends come across my old newspaper cuttings they are, with good reason, appalled. 'How could you *ever* have thought such awful things, Sal, let alone write them *publicly* for other women to read!' But sometimes I wonder if in *their* pasts too there might in some of their self-righteous speeches have been a tiny right-off chink!

When two friends of mine, one a Revolutionary Feminist, one a Socialist Feminist, both said firmly to me: 'I don't think I ever reflect men,' I looked very impressed but I thought: it's not me

21

they are deceiving, it is themselves. Because we all do it. I think the woman who doesn't register that it *is* what she is doing, must be putting a lot of energy into rationalising the process.

It is as hard to get feminist credentials by saying you don't reflect men, as it is by saying you aren't sexist, because our whole society is based on those principles. There are no exceptions. The more women protest they don't, the more they reveal they don't understand what they are doing. What we all do. For when it comes to reflecting men, *feminists are not immune*. Like it or not, they can be found with the other women charging obligingly across factory floors; deferentially womaning the cash tills at Sainsbury's; emptying the coffee cups in school staffrooms; smiling their air-hostess-like smiles as they offer the gin and tonics; dryly delivering unthreatening academic lectures in the great halls of Cambridge and Oxford; tiptoeing in and out of oppressors' bedrooms whispering: 'It doesn't matter. I know you didn't mean to hit me. Of course I still love you.'

This might help to explain why so many books have been written about women's silences and so few about women's speech. About the precise ways they speak *to* men as compared with the precise ways they speak *about* men. About what it is women feel compelled to say when even one man is present, and what they omit saying until they are on their own.

The problem is that because women are encouraged by both sexes to speak to men in this adoring way, male virtues become fraudulently enhanced and male values speciously highlighted in a way that makes their ideas seem not only enviable but also correct, even universal. It was not only in my public life that I reflected men. Reflecting men seemed to be an occupational hazard with me. And one of my occupations at that time was marriage. I did it not once, but twice.

In between, I had several longstanding 'solid' relationships with men. In so doing, I again illustrated another of those contradictions that at twenty I was prey to. Adrienne Rich (1979) points out that 'women have been forced to lie for survival to men' (p.189). Certainly this was true for me. At sixteen, I knew quite clearly that I loved women. I also knew that that way lay danger. I was not, in my teens, the risk taker I am today.

I agree with Gloria Steinem (1984) that 'women may be the one group that grows more radical with age' (p.212). She argues that women in general don't begin to challenge the politics of our own lives until later. Certainly this pattern ran through my life. After college I was insecure and uncertain about my sexuality. No one, it seemed, was like me. Intuitively I knew that to 'succeed' (a misnomer for a concept I would now call 'fail') and to be approved of and loved by family, friends, colleagues and, yes, even passing strangers, I needed to prioritise men. I had to deal with them on their terms. Play by their rules. Moreover I *wanted* to. It wasn't the clash it seems today in retrospect. More than wanting to be honest with myself I wanted to do it all *right*. And 'doing it right' meant having a job but making sure it didn't conflict with getting married and staying married. If that failed, trying to get it right the second time (I am nothing if not persevering) by having children, being an amazing cook and superb housewife. In other words not merely doing it right but doing it wonderfully, and making sure the men at home and at work felt extremely lucky to have me around.

When I had just left university I married for the first time to an eager young journalist. My husband was a benevolent Fleet Street night editor, several years older than I was, who eventually became a reasonably high-ranking civil servant.

Between Fleet Street and the civil service, he went off to Oxford University as a mature student. Going to Oxbridge had been the unfulfilled dream of his northern working-class boyhood: he'd managed the tea-boy-to-night-editor fantasy but he still longed to study amidst the spires. His dream became a reality I helped to foster.

Partly, he got to Oxford through his own untiring efforts, his academic zeal and his genuine abilities. Partly, he got to Oxford because I spent the time between cleaning our flat, cooking our meals and writing my own newspaper articles, coaching him in English literature and Oxford entrance material, offering him the sympathy, persuasive assurances and the confidence he lacked.

All of these are the expert skills of the adult tutor (or the ordinary wife) for which I now charge a reasonable rate. I suppose he was the first of what have been a series of initially unconfident but ultimately successful mature students. Teaching him, talking to him, spending hours of time with him and helping him to work towards what became an important joint goal is certainly something I am very proud to have been a part of. It is not something I either regret or resent. It is merely interesting to observe that what I did for affection and as a proper and considered part of my marriage contract, is also a good illustration of how similar I was to many women who reflect their men in ways calculated to ensure those men succeed. Hiding or minimising any failures he had, encouraging, boosting, sympathising, flattering, spending most of my available time on this project also meant squeezing my own public career and certainly my private writing into the tight and tiny corners between marking my husband's latest essay and throwing together another exciting meal.

In *The Female Eunuch* Germaine Greer says that 'as soon as we find ourselves working at being indispensable, rigging up a pattern of vulnerability in our loved ones, we ought to know that our love has taken the socially sanctioned form of egotism. Every wife who slaves to keep herself pretty, to cook her husband's favourite meals, to build up his pride and confidence in himself at the expense of his sense of reality, to be his closest and effectively his only friend, to encourage him to reject the consensus of opinion and find reassurance only in her arms is binding her mate to her with hoops of steel that will strangle them both' (p.160). Implicit in these lines is the crucial point that building up a man's pride and confidence in this way may also be at the expense of *her* sense of reality.

This is what happened to me. In that first marriage, because I had an independent working existence, I did to some extent preserve my own identity; and the reasons I fell into male reflection were I felt *positive* ones. I felt caring and protective towards this kind man. I also felt guilty because I could not apparently love him in the way he expected. In ways that were important to whatever I believed then was the 'real me', this man could not build me up or increase my confidence. *But I could do that for him.* With goodwill and understanding on both sides. Ironically, it was through suffocation from goodwill that my identity began to be stifled. I couldn't have traced the stages of this process nor probably understood if anyone had analysed it for me. I did, however, have enough sense of survival to get out.

Having spent much of my adult life trained in the ways of getting on better with men because I was adept at manipulating their susceptibilities, their ill-concealed desires and their well-founded guilts, by the time of my second marriage I was already broken by the patriarchy, both as a writer and as a woman. My growing left-wing radical views could not survive intact on a rabid right-wing journal; my growing need to express my secret sexuality could not survive the labels that deemed me sick and vicious. I had to assume that my real identity would come from the man I married not from the work I did, nor from the woman I was. *It remained for me to find an appropriate man to live through.* Someone who would appreciate my skilful reflective services. Germaine Greer says that 'woman shows her own value to her sisters by choosing a successful and personable man' (p.159). I came across one in the course of my work. He was thirty years older than me, a well-known musician who fitted Greer's point that 'women too bask in the reflected glory of their chosen mates. It would be nonsensical to marry a celebrated and artistic man while remaining indifferent to his achievement . . . everyone wants to be recognized and rewarded' (p.159). I was well trained to offer recognition and reward. I was not indifferent to his achievements. I became his personal assistant. Ironically, it was on my very last assignment as a full-time journalist that I met him. He was the assignment. The now defunct but then lively, glossy *Queen* magazine sent me to interview him. In his autobiography he says: 'Sally was bright, funny, extremely clever.' In an interview with a newspaper journalist on our wedding day he said, 'She was such a good listener I knew I had to retain her.' Surprising as it seems now, at the time it was not at all difficult to throw up my career as a journalist and start a new one: first as his assistant then as his publicist, his mistress and finally, his wife, the mother of his child, the manager of his shows and concerts.

All these diverse occupations were built largely around the premise that part of my job was to protect, boost and flatter him. Like most women I knew, I had been brought up to bathe in the reflected glory of my husband's achievements. The more I could promote him, the glossier I looked myself. What was different about my second marriage was that (a) I was paid a small sum weekly to look after my husband and his career, and (b) the care was never reciprocated. When I was his personal assistant I received £12 a week. Later, when I managed his/our money as well as him I paid myself more, with his approval. Not a great deal more: my wages for services always remained well within the expectations of the female service industry. I felt I was lucky to work for such a talented man.

For his performances on stage and in concert halls, I wrote his shows and stage-managed or directed many of his performances. I promoted him larger than life. I also helped with his children from his first marriage and, later, brought up our own daughter. On the posters and in the programmes his name was in large flashy bright-coloured 'caps'. My name was always in neat small black print. I existed as his tenacious and hardworking shadow. I dealt with any problems and tried to smooth the professional paths. I was rarely unhappy. Indeed, I felt very clever to be doing the right thing at last. *In some inexplicable way I knew I had never felt more feminine.* In his autobiography he expresses admiration for me and describes me as a hardworking person. But there is one contradiction to the facts as I lived them: he refers to me as a journalist and yet I'd stopped writing when we met; he never refers to me as a stage director or publicist and yet these were the jobs I held for the length of our relationship. Perhaps his status is greater if he appears to succeed entirely by his own efforts.

Germaine Greer maintains that 'every time a woman makes herself laugh at her husband's often told jokes she betrays him.' More to the point, she betrays herself. This, of course, was not something that was written down in our marriage contract. The rules were there, nevertheless. Laugh at his jokes. Always. Laugh harder the third time around. Listen to him practise. Not often, but that was because he did not like practising. Encourage him to practise. Very often. Reason as before. Worry about his small audiences and large bills. Try to increase the first and decrease the second. Comfort. Nurture. Agree. Rarely, if ever, criticise. Above all follow Forster's dictum, 'Attention must be paid'.

In the early period, my own guilt was the most compelling motive. Later, as an angry, aggressive, non-conforming woman, I learnt that violence could well be the outcome of my failure to make a man feel good. I became aware of the economic implications too. For the first time I did not have my own money. I was a partner; moreover, I was the junior partner in money matters.

Because male reflection is the language of the oppressed, the behaviour of the powerless and the style of the weak, it is clear that being part of a powerless group, all women must reflect men some of the time. But certain groups of women do it more often than others. Women are more likely to reflect men: if they have men's children; if they're brought up to believe that reflection leads to a harmonious home; if frightened of losing promotion or child custody or male approval; of inciting male violence; or, perhaps the main reason, if they are economically dependent.

We are forced to acknowledge that there is a strong material basis for this kind of behaviour: when men earn 90% of the world's wealth, women are not in a position to ignore men's demands.

It is feasible to argue that men who feel good pay more, which provides another reason why women work hard at making men feel good. This work which takes incalculable time and energy and which *all* women acknowledge they do, is not of course mentioned within the masculist economic framework. Yet it is the kind of work which enables the male supremacist system to keep going. And like most women's work it goes both unacknowledged and unpaid.

Why, in the light of these facts, has this problem – which has helped to lock women's experience into a system which depends for its survival on the exploitation of women as homemakers, as sex objects and as submissive, dependent pillars of the nuclear family – lain buried and unacknowledged for so long?

The problem of reflecting men has had no label, precisely and specifically because it has not been a problem for men. As long as I was locked into my job, my marriages and my need for male approval, into accepting dominant values and living earnestly by masculist and heterosexist standards, it was not a problem for me, either. The problems were encountered when I began to question these standards, and in so doing questioned the usefulness of systematically building up male egos while allowing my own brittle identity to be splintered further. The only contradiction in my writing life was that for two years after work, and every weekend, I would write hard and long into the night. I struggled with my first novel in which the loosely concealed middle-class, married heroine painfully comes out as a lesbian and offers her emotional allegiance to women in a society which forbids her to define her own sexuality if she wants to 'succeed'. The heroine's choices, as I recall, were to lose her woman love, to lose her well-meaning, benign husband or to lose her balance. To some extent she lost all three. In those days it was difficult to write about women loving women when that love was either denied or declared deviant. The only hope was in adaptation; revolution was not on the cards, I'm afraid. In better households, homosexuality was regarded as a failure to learn and my heroine like myself, was a fast learner. Significantly, the novel was entitled *The Two*; not surprisingly, it was labelled 'talented' by several publishers but never published.

2

FROM AN EARLY AGE

In 1909, Cicely Hamilton wrote that 'the belief of the average man in his own intellectual superiority . . . is a constant source of worry and petty hindrance' (p.101) to women. Now it's not easy to appear always intellectually superior – as every teacher can testify – so if it is mandatory for men to be seen to know more it's more than likely that women are playing games. The games of 'keeping up appearances'.

For if men feel the need to appear more capable and competent in comparison with women, and if women are concerned to fulfil this need, then the surest and quickest way is for women to give way. If men seek to look bright then women can assist them by feigning foolishness. This is one reason why, from their earliest infancy, women learn to hide their lights under a bushel, to step back so that men appear more prominent and positive.

And this is what Cicely Hamilton was referring to. It is the practice of keeping themselves in check, the habit of toning down their talents so that men can shine and expand which becomes a daily inhibition in women's lives.

What would women be like without this self-imposed constraint? This was the question asked by Cicely Hamilton – playwright, novelist and early-twentieth-century feminist – who was fascinated by the possible forms that femaleness could take if women were permitted to grow to maturity without having to monitor their existence so that it served to enhance the appearance and achievement of men. 'Such a generation [of women] at present is a matter of pure guesswork,' she admitted. And today, we can still only guess what women would be like if they were free to please themselves instead of having to please men.

But if Cicely Hamilton was one of the few females to raise in print the issue of the extent to which women's growth and development have been hampered by the need to promote positive images of man, she is by no means the only one to be familiar with the fetters. Most women are conscious of the constraints which accompany femininity.

We were surprised to find just how many women were aware that they had been treated differently from their brothers. We had not expected such open and ready acknowledgement of the requirement to be the appreciative and encouraging audience for male achievement. All the women we spoke to, regardless of socio-economic status or ethnic background, reported having had to learn that they were less important. For most it was a lesson they never forgot.

Whether it was bed-making or being tidy, sisters did the work so that brothers were kept in a good mood. Whether it was proposing the toasts at family parties or being praised for sporting performances, it was sisters who took the back seat. According to many women, it was soon second nature for sisters to take second place.

Such reports from sisters are illuminating for they constitute part of the evidence that *all* females are required to stand aside for *all* males. It is not just a matter of women deferring to the men on whom they are dependent or even of enhancing the existence of the man they love. For this is the relationship of brother and sister and from it we find that from their infancy females are taught to give way to all males.

So many women we spoke to had been saddened by the fact that their mothers treated them with less tolerance than their brothers. Expressions such as 'She got impatient with us girls' and 'If I was upset I was being bad-tempered, but if my brother was upset there was an inquisition to find out who had caused it' were common in the responses. 'She always spent more time with the boys even when they were at potty stage' was a frequent comment of Teresa's – an Irish Catholic who was one of eleven children, five boys and six girls. 'It wasn't that we felt unwanted, but the girls knew what we were wanted for, and that was cleaning up after the boys. Of course, we had to help with all the babies; food and toilet training, I mean. Mum couldn't look after that lot and there were three of us girls at the top and then all the boys. Then the three little sisters. And we soon knew to take the bottle or dummy away from the girls a lot quicker than from the boys. It was the same with the pot. If they did anything in it, even by accident, it was all congratulations and aren't you a good lad. Whereas if one of the little girls did it, even after an effort, it was "Clear up after that horrid mess one of you and be fast about it" and no praise at all.'

It seems that tidiness is one of the dividing lines. Well, it's called 'tidiness' but it could just as easily be referred to as but another name for work. Girls were expected to be tidy which meant they were expected to *work* in the home while boys were permitted to be untidy which meant they were allowed to *play*, usually outside the home.

Girls were expected to provide services and there wasn't any doubt about who the services were for. Girls got a double load while boys were frequently left free. Girls got to tidy up after boys and to keep themselves tidy as well. If they didn't do the boys' share they were called lazy: if they didn't do their own share they were called shameful or indecent. Such elaborate mechanisms make it appear normal for the boys to be able to play happily while the girls are doing the dishes.

We found that, for girls, tidiness was linked to cleanliness. Again, the success stakes were high. That cleanliness is next to godliness might no longer be the general rule but that cleanliness is next to *good*liness for girls is difficult to deny. One condition of a female's existence seems to be that she should keep all germs away.

Not only are women expected to banish all bacteria from their person, they are also held responsible for the cleanliness of the hearth and home. The frequency with which women recounted being coerced into some form of 'cleanliness' was remarkable. And so many of their reports were extraordinary, indeed they even bordered on the bizarre.

This facet of female training has not escaped the attention of theorists and writers. In her book *Little Girls*, Elena Belotti argues that in terms of cleanliness, 'mothers are more demanding of their daughters than their sons' (p.41). Her interviews led her to conclude that 'mothers are also more tolerant of little boys when they soil their pants (even grown men are thought of as being naturally dirty) than of little girls. The latter are expected to make as few demands as possible, to be clean, careful, and to look after their appearance and their own bodies. Of course such a degree of self-control is only achieved later on but the goal is constant from the start. Indeed its existence is essential for producing the required feminine behaviour. If a boy is dirty and untidy this seems the natural order of things. If a girl is, she is looked upon as an annoyance and is attributed with the malicious intention of not wanting to keep herself clean. "She does it on purpose" the mother will say' (1975, p.42).

"CLEVER BOY!"

Until we began to interview women we thought that Elena Belotti could have been overstating the case. But now we can corroborate her statements. We found that girls are consistently being taught that they are not allowed to be dirty and they are also taught that it doesn't matter if boys are. Girls are told that it is unpardonable for them to be dirty ('There's nothing worse than a dirty woman' was the predominant and painful injunction from one woman's past) but that it is understandable when boys are. So females shouldn't make a fuss: it's a woman's job to get rid of the dirt – to make everything shining bright and clean. No wonder analysis and advertising agencies can have a field day with women's fears and phobias about dirt and contamination. But one does wonder why there is so little attention paid to the origin of this phenomenon.

Gill's was a typical recollection. 'I can remember being embarrassed,' she told us, and could not prevent herself from blushing again. She spoke slowly and her account was punctuated by painful pauses: 'I was upset for days. I'd had my period and I'd put my knickers in the dirty clothes, you see, and when my mum was sorting them out, to do the washing, well she just marched straight in and held my knickers up in front of everyone. "What's this mess? I'm not your slave, you know!" And I can still remember how awful I felt. She just threw them down on the floor. I had to pick them up. My brother used to hold his nose for weeks when he came near me. Oh god . . . it was so awful.

'But you know, *his* pants were often soiled. I helped to sort the washing too, and he really was a dirty bastard. I used to think about what would happen if I'd ever thrown his filthy pants in the middle of the sitting-room floor. I'd have been thrown out, I suppose. My mum would never have forgiven me. She didn't do that to Dad either. You just don't do it to boys.'

Why do women treat their daughters like this? Gill's account of being shamed was not unusual. Perhaps mothers are passing on a lesson they have learnt: 'binding the feet' of their daughters in the same way that they were deformed themselves. Is it an unthinking perpetuation of what they themselves were taught or something more insidious which ensures that their daughters learn early exactly what is expected of them later? That they will do the shit work: that it is their lot in life.

For Cicely Hamilton, these lessons that girls learnt were in the nature of 'atrocities' and like footbinding itself, Cicely Hamilton explained them in terms of the 'marriage market'.

In households where mothers see the happiness of their daughters residing in relationships with men, it is the good mother who can insist on the daughter's conformity so that she will be attractive to the right man. Even when she can see that her daughter is being hurt, she can still rationalise that it is what men like, it is what men want and so it is what men will get. No matter what price the daughter must pay or the indignity she must suffer, it is worth the prize.

Is this not the message in the tale of *Cinderella*? Where the 'good' mother encourages the stepsisters to cut off part of their feet in order that the slipper might fit? That women should be 'deformed' to be acceptable to men is a belief which runs right through our society. It is a belief which makes it plausible for women to *reduce* themselves to appeal to men. A belief which encourages mothers to be responsible for such reductions.

This is another aspect of socialisation that would have to change if we were to answer Cicely Hamilton's question of what women would look like if they were allowed to please themselves. For while ever mothers teach their daughters what they themselves were taught there is no way out of the 'vicious circle' in which women learn to please men. We have heard much lately about how salvation lies in women's treatment of their sons; perhaps it would be more profitable to look at the way women rear their daughters. Perhaps we could begin to ask why girls have again taken second place, with the emphasis in the literature on child-rearing being placed on women's attitude to their sons.

Many mothers have a lot to answer for in the way that they have circumscribed the aspirations and achievements of their daughters. And some daughters have explained – and even forgiven – the awful things that were done to them 'for their own good'. 'My mother did the best that she could for me in terms of what she knew,' one woman said without rancour as she recounted the rigid and restrictive practices of her early years. 'When my mother made me curl my hair and diet – and insisted that I learn to do embroidery as well as cleaning and cooking – she wasn't trying to hurt me, though that's certainly what she did,' said Greta, a welder and a member of Women in Manual Trades. 'She just wanted me to be successful, and as a woman that was what you had to do.'

Most women recall being prevented or persuaded from breaking free from some of the constraints of femininity. Most women are aware of the double standard – and incensed at its injustice – which prescribes one rule for women and another for men. And we found very few women who remembered their mothers assuring them that they were as important as their brothers. Rather, even when the daughters were seen to be more talented, even when they were held to be brighter and were more concerned to continue their education, it was still the sons who were seen to deserve it more.

'The toughest part was working out that it didn't matter how well I did in school,' Emily told us in tones still tinged with bitterness. 'My mother insisted that we could only afford one student in the family, and that it wasn't going to be me. It was to be my brother. As soon as I was old enough, I had to get a job, to help out. And it was really my pay that was providing my brother's pocket money. And he wasn't a bit interested in learning. He failed, two years running. And he didn't think it was unfair that I was the one who wanted to go to university but couldn't, that I was the one who had to get a job so he could go. And so he could fail.'

Emily did not abandon her own ambitions but attended evening classes in order to study for her A levels. Her eventual success was hard won: 'It was bloody difficult really. I got no support at all at home. I went to work, then to classes, and when I got home my mother made sure I didn't get out of any of my chores. I'd be really tired and just getting started on an essay or something and she'd be on about the dishes not all being done or the bathroom not being properly clean. Sometimes the things she got me up for were so petty I wondered whether she was really trying to stop me from doing any studying. And that's not an exaggeration. I think she thought I was showing my brother up. She resented me getting on while he didn't. So finally I left home – not just because she was all for my brother, though I found that hard at the time – but because I had a lot more time to study when I left.

'But you know, my mother never congratulated me when I got my degree. She wanted a successful son. And a *married* daughter, with children. Now it's the other way round. And I'm sure she thinks that somehow it's my fault.'

Only Emily's experience is quoted here but many other accounts were very much like hers. Virtually every woman who had a brother reported being required to take second place when it came to education. 'It's more important for a boy' and 'It's only wasted on a girl' were among the words of wisdom which women said were bestowed on them when young. 'You'll only waste it and get married' was the response a cross-section of women said they had received when they registered an interest in continuing their education.

Some women were adamant that they would not make the same mistake of handing on such advice to their own daughters. They regretted their own absence of training and the paucity of employment opportunities. They were determined that their daughters should do better than they had done. With such resolutions from mothers and self-professed hopes for their daughters, one could be forgiven for leaping to the conclusion that great changes are going on. For we didn't have to look far to find women who were putting their faith in their daughters' future in education and employment, as well as marriage. Most mature women were convinced that wives should have something more than a man as their livelihood and preoccupation.

Women 'needed a job to fall back on when the children left home' we were told. And more perfunctorily and plaintively, women needed a job to fall back on if the husband left home! But women also needed jobs to take them outside the home: women also needed jobs for interest. We never heard a woman say that a man needed work – as an interest.

So even as women talked of equipping their daughters with resources which they thought they had been denied themselves, we found that the doubts could creep in. For are mothers adopting a single standard for their children, or a double one which again allows the advantage to the men? It did not seem to us that mothers were always teaching their daughters that they had the same rights to education and employment as their sons. On the contrary, even where women were encouraging their daughters to take up education and employment it was generally in a context which quite clearly did not challenge men.

Far from teaching daughters that they were free to try anything in which they were interested and to aim as high as it was possible to go, many mothers were suggesting the practicality of a pleasant job or a 'little career' which posed no threat to men. We found that there was a reluctance, even resistance, to the idea of treating the educational and employment needs of women as the same as men's. Even where women were actually pushing their daughters to think in terms of training and paid work, it was sometimes couched in terms of the 'attractiveness' of their incomes to a man (who would not have the sole responsibility as breadwinner) rather than as positive independence for themselves.

In comparison with their own mothers, women today may have made educational and employment gains but in comparison with their brothers things are much the same as for centuries they have been. In education and employment women are still being taught to take second place to men.

'I know my daughter's bright and I'll do all I can to help her with her education – but I don't want her to be a career woman,' said Meg, who was extremely critical of the way her own mother had made her look to marriage rather than paid work as her means of support. 'A well-paid job, that's what she needs. But not one that puts a man off. A good job *and* a good husband. Not one of these women who puts her job before everything, because really, the family still has to come first. And she'll still have to think about *his* job. Maybe she'll have to do entertaining for him, or pack up and go with him when he moves. That's why she needs something you can take up anywhere. And she's going to get her training for it. Not like me.'

But is this such an improvement? Is it not just a new version of the old principle that women should give way so that men can appear more important? Is this not just another example of women reining in their own resources in order to give full and favoured play to those of men? We did wonder what Meg's daughter would think of Meg's attitude in future years: would she in turn make the same criticisms as Meg had made of *her* mother?

Girls have been – and still are – continually cajoled and coerced into making it look as though boys are in charge. For the majority of women this was the most persuasive lesson of their past and even though they often spoke with resentment about such restrictions, we had to conclude, regrettably, that they were frequently imparting a comparable lesson to their daughters. By both blatant and subtle means most mothers made sure that girls learnt the necessity of not eclipsing boys: not in daily life, not in achievements, not in future careers.

Glenda was one woman who had learnt early that though her brother was younger, and to all intents and purposes 'powerless' – 'He was in nappies, I ask you!' – she still had to give way to him. With some resentment she reported that any expression of her interest was seen to be interference with the flowering of her brother.

'I was supposed to look after him,' she said, 'but really that meant that I was supposed to indulge him, let him do what *he* liked, as long as he didn't get into any trouble. If I wanted to go to the park but he wanted to do something else then I would be *dominating*, I would be bossy if we did what I wanted. He wasn't called dominating when we did what he wanted . . . which was all the time.'

Glenda went on to say that this was when she learnt that men didn't have to have money or power to get their own way: 'It was just enough to be a boy. There I was changing my brother's nappy

– and having to do what he wanted to do. As if something dreadful would happen to him if he were thwarted! No wonder men can't cope with not getting their own way,' she added, 'they haven't had any practice. They can be tyrants even before they are toilet-trained.'

While we had no way of determining whether Glenda's daughter was enjoined to indulge her brother, we did discover that the daughter – who was a year younger than the son – was considered to be more responsible and accountable. But we also discovered that Glenda was not alone in making such an assessment of the earlier 'maturity' of girls. And we did discover that by holding girls to be more 'mature' than boys it is possible for mothers – and society – to rationalise that girls can see the good sense of taking second place to boys. This concept that girls have greater control over themselves than boys, from an earlier age, seems to be part of the socialisation process that *checks* the development of girls and encourages the development of boys.

What effect does it have, though, when at such a young age girls come to understand that they are unacceptable if they cannot let it be seen that boys are in charge? There are no systematic studies which document the price paid by girls in the loss of self-esteem. There are no long-term research projects which analyse the consequences of being required to sacrifice one's self – or which examine the punishment handed out to women who persist with being 'selfish'. Despite the fact that the majority of the population is being 'programmed' in this particular way, as a society we know little or nothing about the results to the psyche from such habitual treatment. Could this be why so many more women than men suffer from mental illness?

What we do know is that in our society it is normal for girls to be taught from their infancy that they do not count as much as boys. We know that it is normal for sisters to be taught at home that they must willingly and cheerfully take second place to their brothers. We know that it is made incumbent on females to help to project males in a positive light even if it is at considerable cost to themselves. We know that this is the relationship between the sexes that is shaped in children and used in adulthood.

Nan, twenty-eight, a lab technician, talked to us freely, but was unwilling to try and pinpoint where she had learnt to inflate the image of men. This, she explained, was because for her whole life she had listened to her father and her brother blaming her mother for everything that went wrong and she didn't want to join the family club by saying it was all her mother's fault. But, she admitted ruefully, her mother had certainly impressed upon her that it was a fundamental rule of life for females to reflect men at twice their size.

'Looking back, I realise it was my mum – and my aunties – who were always teaching me how to get round men. Not that they said it like that, of course. It was more what they did. 'Cos my brother was never asked to help – and I was, all the time. His time was seen as precious. Mine was not seen as important. I was always supposed to be ready to help Dad or Charlie. No one even thought that it was interrupting . . .'

Nan continued: 'The thing I remember was about the decorating. I did all the boring things. Dad and Charlie did all the interesting stuff. "Get this Nan," my dad would say, and "Yes, you go and help Dad and Charlie," my mother would tell me. And my aunt would say not to be difficult about it. "We want it all to go smoothly," Mum would go on, "Don't get the men upset." '

There was no doubt that Nan's experience still rankled: 'Dad took down the centre wall and made a through room, and Mum wanted them to be decorated the same colour. She had a lot of taste, my mum. But Dad said they had to be different coloured to keep their character. They didn't have different characters though – and I said so. Then there was trouble – wouldn't you know it? "Don't upset your father, Nan, he knows what he's doing." I tried to persuade Mum to say what she felt about the colour scheme but she wouldn't stand up to him. She wouldn't even tell Charlie, my brother. She just kept saying it was best to agree with the men because they didn't like it if you didn't go along with them. "It makes them feel ordinary instead of big," she used to say. So you can see where I learnt it all.'

Whether girls are instructed directly by rules or indirectly by 'models' provided by mothers or aunts, what girls are learning is that it is 'law' that the well-being of boys should always be promoted: that the psychical and physical needs of boys should be met by girls. And nowhere is this more apparent than it is with the housework.

The rate at which boys are released from responsibility in this area is well recorded. Not that this means there is outrage or even a sense of injustice registered when it is revealed just how much work ends up in the hands of girls – and how little in the hands of

boys. When confronted with some of the startling statistics –
supplied by everything from the EEC* to *Good Housekeeping* – the
response of many is simply to shrug and state, *'What do you
expect, boys will be boys!'*

Such resignation is not always so readily cultivated among the
young, however, as Angela McRobbie (1978) found when she
interviewed working-class adolescent girls. She repeatedly
quotes girls who recognised that they were required to be
responsible for the housework while their brothers were seen to
have 'better' things to do: 'Me brother doesn't do a thing in the
house. He makes a mess and I clear up after him. He doesn't even
make his own bed, waits for me mum to do it when she gets in
from work,' said Jill, one of Angela McRobbie's interviewees
(p.100). Like so many other young women Jill might have been
resentful but, like so many other young women, coming to accept
that it was her role to clean up after men was a lesson she could
not fail to learn.

It is much easier to act and appear superior when one does not
have to deal with the dreary details of everyday life. It is much
easier to stride through the world and look like someone of note
when there is no need to think on the disorder left behind. It is
much easier to be expansive when one is carefree.

It is much harder to be confident and courageous when one
must clean up the mess. It is much harder to have presence and
panache when one must pick up the pieces and remove any signs
of pollution.

Among the women to whom we spoke who were trying to cut a
daring and dashing figure in the world, was a young punk from
the King's Road in Chelsea. Seemingly assertive and independent, giving the impression of being bold and free, the tale she
told of life at home showed just how difficult it could be for girls.

'Me and my brother, well, we haven't got jobs. And me mum's
biggest worry is that he don't have enough pocket money – and
might do something silly – and that I don't do enough at home. So
she's always trying to give him extra. And she's always on at me
to stay and mind the house. And to keep an eye out for him, I
think. We have a lot of rows. I think she just wants me to be in all
day and doing the housework. While she's out working for my
brother's pocket money! I get sorry for her sometimes. She works

* See Mary Ingham, 1984.

hard and he's not a bit grateful. Why should he be? He gets to have this great life and no responsibility. And me mum wants me to have no life at all.'

She admitted that only on two days a week was she allowed to leave the house. 'But that's not too bad,' she said with a wry grin. 'Takes a full day to do me hair so I could only get out every second day anyway.'

Such a sense of humour in circumstances that were distressing (and at times even desperate) was by no means unusual. For us there was something rather disconcerting about being able to laugh when so much of what we were being told was so shocking. But there was a form of 'gallows humour' among women when they talked of the way of – and the reasons for – reflecting men.

All the women we talked to had something to say about the manner in which they had been taught to reflect men when they were children. (Some said they wouldn't be prepared to talk about it in public – to be taped – because it was unfair to their mothers: some because they thought it was unfair to men.) But without exception women made it abundantly clear that they did not feel free to choose their own ways of responding to men. They were adamant that they were required in all sorts of situations – at

"It's a new baby brother for you to help look after."

home, at work, in bed, on the street, at parties, in pubs, with men they knew and men they didn't know, with men on whom they were dependent and men on whom they were not – to make men feel bigger, more important, more assured and hence happier with their world and their place within it. Where women differed was in that some regretted or resented this much more than others.

3

SCHOOLING FOR SUBORDINATION

At home girls learn the pervasive lesson of the importance of putting boys first, but home is not the only place where instruction in this art occurs. Schools also make a considerable contribution in coaching girls to take second place. And within educational institutions there are two basic means by which girls are taught to see themselves as servers of men.

The first is the more explicit. For there have been and still are courses which have been expressly devised to prepare girls for future service. Such courses (like home economics) have been 'modified' in recent times to remove some of the more blatant manifestations of inequality, but their continued existence still helps to emphasise that the two sexes are intended for two very different roles in life, and that one role carries with it more privileges and power than the other.

The second means by which students are taught is less direct: sometimes referred to as the area of the 'hidden curriculum', this form of instruction is in the realm of expectation, the realm of example or 'modelling', where the aims and directions often go unstated. Whether this is the more powerful form of imparting knowledge it is difficult to tell, but it is a form of which most women appear to be conscious in relation to their own education.

When we asked women what they had learnt at school or college about reflecting men, they tended to talk about both the direct and indirect ways in which they had been taught to reduce their own achievements and to boost those of boys.

'When someone important came to the school,' Belinda said in reference to primary education about twenty years ago, 'boys got to make the speeches and girls got to make the tea. So we spent our time in the kitchen thinking about looking after the speakers and the guests. And the boys got to be looked after. From the day I started school the girls were expected to be the audience for boys. And the waitresses. And "cleaner-uppers". The school definitely taught us that.' It seems that school still teaches this lesson to girls. Some teachers, some mothers – and some girls – are acutely critical of such a curriculum.

Barbara is a 'home-ecs' teacher who over the last ten years has put a lot of energy into trying to change her subject 'from within'. But she admits that is beyond the resources of one teacher – or the resources of a small group of teachers – to reverse the traditional philosophy of a subject or to re-educate the staff and students in what might be done. 'No matter how hard we try,' she said, 'home economics can still be used to reinforce women's subordination. It can still be used as the subject that teaches women how to look after men.'

It was one of her greatest disappointments that the entry of boys into the class had not resulted in both sexes' assuming equal responsibility for their daily needs: 'It wasn't just that the boys said they thought it was a good idea to learn to cook – in case their wife got ill, or they found they *had* to do it,' Barbara said with more than a hint of disgust. 'It's that some of the bloody teachers – and a lot of the girls – make such a fuss about the boys who *do* attend. Aren't they *good* boys to be so thoughtful and responsible,' she said with mimicry. 'It's the best ego-boost the boys can get being praised like that. And it's a real "chef versus cook" syndrome too. I just about go bonkers when I find the girls cutting up the vegetables and cleaning up, while the boys swan around doing the creative culinary bit. *And* they get thanked for it.'

These were not the limits of Barbara's objections to the established and endorsed school subject of home economics. She was also deeply distressed by elements of the course known as 'personal grooming', which were applied almost exclusively to girls. To Barbara this was just another way in which the school explicitly taught (and examined!) ways for women to be pleasing to men. So depressed was she by her work, she was thinking of resigning: 'If home ecs was teaching boys how to take care of girls – or how to appeal to girls and be attractive to girls – it would be a different matter,' she said. 'But all it's doing is preparing girls to clean up after men. And to meet their emotional needs. And I can't teach that – and stay sane.'

Barbara did not object to the fact that students were being taught to cut up vegetables: nor did she object to lessons in coiffures, cosmetics and clothes *per se*. What she was objecting to was that such skills were considered appropriate for just one sex.

When an examination is made of the implications of this 'one rule for women and another for men', then the very different status of the sexes is soon exposed. For example, there would be a scandal if boys were required to become proficient at 'personal grooming' and fashion, partly because such learning would be considered a veritable waste of the valuable time of boys. It would be assumed that *as they were boys* they had more important things to learn at school. Boys are being prepared for a place in the world, so personal grooming – while undeniably desirable – is not a priority. But for girls who are being prepared to find, get, and keep boys, everything from personal grooming to household hints can be part of the trade. Which is why it is not thought to be a waste to devote educational time to developing these attributes in girls.

While Barbara was the most outspoken (and disillusioned) she was not the only critical teacher among the women to whom we talked. This is not surprising, of course: because teaching is considered to be 'a good job for a girl', teaching – like nursing – still constitutes one of the commonest professions for women. (And this is one reason why these professions are so poorly paid: for further discussion see Chapter Six.)

Among the women in education was Sandra, a secondary school teacher, who was more critical of the hidden than the prescribed curriculum, and who was acutely aware of the complications that girls encountered when they tried to make plans for the future. 'First of all,' she said, 'it's not a *simple* question when you ask a girl what she's going to do with her life, because when it comes down to it, how does she know? Because *it all depends* – it depends on who she's going to marry, what *he* will do, where *he* will live, how many children *he* will want. Even whether he's going to allow his wife to work! So how can a girl make any sort of plans for the future when she's still at school and doesn't know the answer to any of these questions?'

Boys, Sandra said, could singlemindedly set their sights on a future for themselves, if they so wished. Society (and some of the

44

mothers we spoke to) would then see it as 'sensible' for the girls to fit into the boys' plans. So, according to Sandra, a girl is in the absurd position of suspending her own plans in the interest of some unknown and future man. 'It's preposterous,' she said. 'A girl subordinates her own aims and aspirations and of course, by doing so, she becomes subordinate.'

Sandra, however, was quick to add that girls should not be blamed for this: 'They're always being told they aren't free to make their own decisions, that they can't suit themselves,' she informed us. 'I've sat in on some of the careers counselling they get, and you can see why they don't rush to commit themselves. Every time a girl says she's thinking of taking up something serious – that she's thinking of entering some profession, or something – she gets asked what she's going to do about the children . . .

'For Chrissake,' Sandra exclaimed, 'they're not even *real* children. They might never exist. But they are what a girl is supposed to plan her life around. And you can see that girls think it's *their* problem. You don't hear anyone asking boys what they are going to do about their non-existent children!'

The way girls were being 'duped' (Sandra's word) was spelt out for us: 'The husband, and the children, they might never come true,' Sandra said exasperatedly. 'A girl might grow up to decide she doesn't want children. Or that she'd rather be lesbian. Worse things could happen,' she added. 'There's always the bomb.'

Whether or not one wanted to go along with Sandra's catalogue of horrors it was hard not to go along with her logic that it was ludicrous for girls to limit their development on the spurious grounds that it was for the sake of the unknown boys and unconceived offspring. Yet she was convinced that this was precisely what girls were doing: they were restricting their options and retarding their own growth because they did not know how acceptable their achievement or independence would be to the men whom they had not yet met. And what Sandra said of schools today seemed to be little different in substance from the recollections many women had of their own schooling – often years ago.

Many of the women we spoke to said they had been channelled away from career and self-development more by indirect than direct means. It was not so much that they had been told they could *not* undertake serious or professional work but that because of all their other commitments it would be very difficult for them and they were discouraged from doing so.

One account, from Alice, is typical of women who, almost thirty years ago, entertained the idea of a university education: 'I always thought I'd like to have a career, to go to university and be quite independent,' she said. 'My marks at school were good enough. I even thought about being a solicitor. I can't say I was told it was impossible, but I soon got the message it wouldn't be easy. All that study. And no money. All that time when you couldn't enjoy yourself, go to parties, buy clothes and things. At least that's what I was led to believe. Being a student looked so dull and dreary and so I had second thoughts about it.'

Not that this was all, she reminded us: 'There was all the talk about the waste of it. That all the training would be wasted on a girl. That all my hard work would be wasted. I would only go and get married. I'd just have children and give it all up. It got so that it just didn't seem worth it.'

Someone suggested to Alice, that, for a girl, it would be better to be a legal secretary than a solicitor. It was advice Alice took and which she has come to regret. 'Now, every day I'm sorry I listened. Every day at work I ask myself why I'm the secretary and not the solicitor. And the answer isn't satisfactory.'

When girls are asked to see their future in terms of marriage and motherhood, and are then urged to prepare themselves for these roles, a vicious circle can soon be constructed: for when they train themselves for domesticity girls often find that they have disqualified themselves from doing much else. It is nothing other than social convenience which dictates the educational agenda of girls and directs them along the straight and narrow path to hearth and home. When it is socially convenient for women to do other things – to do the work men do not *want* to do or cannot do because of war or some other thing – then the education of women and the expectations held of them can undergo immediate and dramatic change.

Historically there have been periods when women have 'gone off the track' and departed from the traditional duties of wife and mother. During the wars, for instance, not only did women do much of the work customarily done by men and for which many of them had been educationally advised that they were ill-fitted; but women also tasted some of the fruits of freedom, freedom from looking after and nurturing men. However, this new-found independence never represented a permanent gain. When the men returned and needed the jobs and the 'comforts of home' (comforts women invariably went without when they performed the work that the men had done) it was once more socially convenient for women to sacrifice their jobs and independence – for the sake of the men. Education played a crucial role in persuading women to give up their gains.

The pendulum swung back swiftly after the Second World War when women were almost swept from the workplace back into the home. They were urged to remember the lessons they had learned and which had been abandoned – regrettably – in the aberration of war. The leading educationalist of the time, John Newsom, made the official recommendation in 1948 that girls in school should 'relearn the graces so many had forgotten' (p.109) and there could be no doubt about what John Newsom considered those graces to be: the graces of managing and pleasing men, which women had forgotten while they had led their independent lives.

Two women to whom we spoke could distinctly recall this period of propaganda on back-to-the-home and what it had meant in their lives: 'I was made to feel ever so guilty for wanting to keep my job,' said Elsie. 'I did *want* to keep it. I did *know* just how much better off I would be with my own money and my own life. I didn't want to be dependent on my husband. But everyone said I was taking it away from a man. That I was being selfish. That it was more important for a man to have a job and his pride. So I left. But it was hard. And I have always been sorry.'

Elsie said she was sorrier when trends changed during the sixties and women were not considered so wilful or selfish for wanting jobs: and she was even sorrier when her husband left her. 'Sometimes it seems to me that giving up my job was the worst thing I ever did,' she acknowledged. 'But then it didn't seem that I had much choice. The pressure was enormous. Things have changed now. I don't think you young ones know just how difficult it could be.'

Have things changed so much? Many of the lessons Elsie learnt (or relearnt) after the Second World War are still being taught today. Women are still being schooled to take second place to men. Moreover, the education of women is predominantly in the hands of men (Eileen Byrne, 1978, estimates that 99% of the government of education is male); surely this is significant?

There is not a woman who does not know that there are men who 'prefer' females who are not too bright. Physical prowess aside, 'intelligence' is the area of greatest possible threat to the male ego.

Some women did know the occasional man who could cope with intelligent women; *all* women knew some men who could not. And this attitude of men has enormous implications for the education of women. As women freely informed us, the girls who pick up the prizes for academic achievement rarely pick up the prizes for popularity from the boys. For adolescent girls – and for women – approval if not popularity among males can become an over-riding concern. After all, it is the area where females are encouraged to see themselves as successes or failures.

Men have always tried to protect themselves from intellectual challenge. In the seventeenth and eighteenth centuries men guarded against the eventuality of being challenged by women by the simple expediency of denying women any opportunities for intellectual development. And in depriving women of education men reaped not one, but two rewards: without education women were in no position to question the wisdom, authority, or superiority of men; similarly, men could argue that women could take no part in public or political life for the very good reason that they were not educated. It is another vicious circle – and it is one with many advantages. While men could keep women from education and public and professional occupation then the very existence of women as untutored and 'untrustworthy' was sufficient in itself to reinforce the male claims of dominance. Because their own capacities were so constrained, whether they liked it or not, or wanted to or not, there is a way in which nineteenth-century (and earlier) women reflected men at twice their normal size. In contrast to women it would not have been hard for men to appear as intellectual giants.

One difficulty for men was that they had to explain why they provided so many opportunities for themselves and so few for women. To justify the restrictions they imposed on women's education they produced one scientific treatise after another which proved that women could not hope to profit from education and that, on the contrary, women would be irreparably harmed by it. The commonest fate they predicted for the educated woman was that her brain would burst, and her uterus would atrophy; understandably, their authoritative pronouncements produced the required results. For even where education was 'technically available' to her, a woman could well be so alarmed by the prospect of pain and poor health that she was more likely to abandon any ideas of pursuing a course of study than to take advantage of the opportunity.

This is where past and present practices have a great deal in common. With both there is the inherent suggestion that women have 'weaknesses' which disqualify them from intellectual training and development: hormones and pre-menstrual tension are the present 'deficiencies' in vogue. And recognition of such debility serves to dissuade women from seeking the same rigorous education and rewards as men.

But if alerting women to their weaknesses is not sufficient to prevent them from entering the world of men, there is still a last resort which has been used in the past and continues to be called on in the present. It is the scare tactic. All the women to whom we spoke had come up against it.

'I was absolutely convinced that if I chose a career, no one would choose me,' said Heather, a successful mature student and now a polytechnic lecturer. 'I just believed all those scare stories – how I would be an old maid. How I'd be lonely and no one would like me. And I decided it wasn't for me . . .

'Do you know I decided against doing medicine because I genuinely believed it would lead straight to a lonely old age?' she told us. 'Sometimes now I don't know whether to laugh or cry at that person I was then – how could I have been so taken in?'

Virtually every woman to whom we spoke had received some version of this grim picture of the fate that lay in store for the self-centred woman. All of them said that it was something that they had to come to terms with and many resented the way such a threat had been used to curb their aspirations.

'The message is pretty simple,' Heather said upon reflection. 'Either you put men first or you get punished. You are made unlovable. You are made unhappy. You become a failure. That's pretty strong stuff and you'd have to really be someone to stand against it. Not many seventeen-year-olds could do it.'

The risk of ending up alone and miserable – because they don't please a man – is one which girls and women are still presented with today. It has become a real fear for many women who can construct a cause-and-effect relationship from some of the contingencies of life, and who think it could well prove to be disastrous to put all their eggs in the one basket of a career. (Of course, that it could prove to be equally if not more disastrous to put all their eggs in the basket of one man is a risk that is not presented in an equally dangerous light.) Some women did not want to take this risk themselves and some did not want their daughters to take it.

'It's not a future I want for my daughter,' Meg said, emphatically. 'I didn't want to end up on my own, with just a career for company. It'd be a miserable life and I wouldn't wish it on any girl. But there's no getting away from it. Girls still need jobs and decent pay. But they can't afford to scare the fellows off. Not if they want a full life. That's why girls have to strike a balance somehow.'

What such a balance should be was difficult to define. Like the girls who were asked what they would be doing as young women, most of the women we asked were inclined to answer in terms of 'it depends': it depends on the man, what the balance would be.

More specific were the responses in relation to success. Women fear success, or at least this was what psychologist Matina Horner concluded when she undertook her study of young women in the 1970s. In her sample she found women who quite explicitly sought educational achievements but who were worried about the consequences of such success. It wasn't just a theoretical consideration that they might be punished for 'achievement'. It was the experience of some of the women in Matina Horner's sample that 'success in public' could well be the precursor to 'failure in private'.

None of the women to whom we talked had been questioned by Matina Horner, but they could have been for there was an overlap and we can corroborate some of her findings. For we spoke with women who were convinced that it was the *advance* at work which was responsible for the *end* of their relationship. Among the group of women (all over thirty) who saw themselves as having a career, it was not uncommon to hear a variation on the theme, 'The better I did at work, the worse he got.' This was Lucy's explanation for the breakdown of her marriage:

'He'd sulk. He'd try and keep me late for work. He'd make plans knowing I couldn't do what he wanted – that I'd have a meeting or something. And sarcastic comments about how he hadn't known I would turn into such a bitch. Finally there was a showdown. He said "Work or me!" '

Lucy chose work in the end. And was one of the women who had no regrets about the decision she had made. 'I figured work had more going for it than he did,' she said somewhat ironically.

But there were other women who regretted and resented the fact that they had been forced to choose, and some who thought that the decision they had made had been a mistake. All of these women felt they had been treated unfairly, not only because they had been confronted with what they thought was an impossible choice (between a career and a family) – and not only because this was a peculiarly female dilemma, but also because they believed that women were punished for being bright and competent. One of the most bitter comments we recorded related to one woman's recognition that she was 'attractive' when helpless, and someone to be repulsed and reviled when she showed signs of intelligence, independence and 'success'.

'Even when it comes to basics, we have to pretend to be stupid and seek help from a man,' Esther said. 'There's no woman who couldn't learn to fix a fuse or change a tyre – but bloody men would feel redundant if that's what women did. So we go round acting helpless and boosting the egos of men. It's enough to make you sick. When will it all end?'

There is not much evidence that such practices are coming to an end. We suspect that currently there are some generational differences with women over thirty who are more directly aware of the penalties women can be required to pay, while younger women are more inclined to think that improvements have been made. But even where younger women do have greater expectations of fair treatment than their mothers may have done, research evidence suggests that they continue to learn many of the same debilitating lessons in school. In the words of the eminent American educationalist, Florence Howe, girls are still learning to be 'silly or silent' in the classroom in order to set up the seeming supremacy of the male.

Some of the younger women (as well as some of the older ones) supported this statement. They had no difficulty in describing the system of rewards and punishments which apply to girls in school. The girl who *knows*, who excels, is frequently scorned by members of both sexes who see her breaking the social code. And her behaviour is seen as even more unfitting – and more open to rebuke – if she 'shows off' in a subject that has been appropriated by the boys. A little more leeway is granted to girls to be good in the less career-oriented subjects (such as art or music*) but when it comes to the more serious and 'professional' areas of science and maths, girls can be made quickly and crudely aware that they are intruding if they are unwise enough to do well.

These 'facts' have even registered with the Department of Education and Science in England where considerable anxiety has been expressed at the dramatic reduction of the performance of girls in maths and science at the onset of adolescence. Girls who have previously been proficient (and who have indicated that they enjoy maths and science) have suddenly failed these subjects, or simply abandoned them.

One result of this withdrawal of girls from the area is that boys, in comparison, look good. Another is that it is boys who leave school better equipped with the qualifications for careers.

Educational authorities have known for some time that there has been a problem about the performance of girls in 'boys' subjects'. It used to be believed that the explanation for the depressed results of girls could be found in the poorer resources provided in girls' schools. This is why mixed-sex education was seen as a solution. For when girls were educated with the boys they would get the same good teachers and facilities and, therefore, do as well as the boys. This was an admission on the part of the educational authorities that they had been practising sex discrimination by providing a poorer education for girls, but their 'solution' has also turned out to be a mistake.

In mixed-sex schools the performance of girls in maths and science has proved to be worse. Fewer girls continued with maths and science when they were educated with boys, as the Department of Education and Science discovered when it conducted its own research (D.E.S., 1975). Despite assurances and protestations to the contrary, despite the widespread belief that progress is being made, all the evidence suggests that women are continuing to conceal their competence in career subjects on a grand scale. This 'under-achievement' of girls has become so staggering that in 1985 it made the British news with the publication of a government-sponsored report.† The report stated that in Britain

* Female competence in these areas does not carry over to the world of paid work of course: how many women artists and musicians have been honoured?

† See review of Barbara Smail's *Girl-Friendly Science* (School Curriculum Development Committee, 1985) in *The Times Higher Education Supplement*, 11 January 1985. p.4.

girls are virtually excluded from all branches of maths and science.

Educational and government officials seemed to express some surprise as to why this should be so. Yet why girls would withdraw from mathematics and science – *en masse* – was no puzzle for the women to whom we spoke. Most did not hesitate to declare that the woman who does well in these fields is found to be unfeminine. For many women, to be unfeminine is to be a failure.

Furthermore, the women we talked to could tell tales of what happened to girls who would not go willingly: they were verbally and sometimes physically harassed. Older women talked of being 'teased' and taunted when they triumphed in traditionally male areas of expertise. Younger women (and mothers in relation to daughters) talked of being forcibly restrained and cited examples such as that of being physically prevented from using the computer. Such evidence is sadly consistent with the findings of systematic research studies (see Elizabeth Fennema, 1980).

When asked why they do badly at maths and science, girls, no more frequently than boys, say it is because they don't like or can't do these subjects. But girls have an additional reason for their poor performance and for dropping out. While they may not give their explanation in explicit terms, and may not always see it as a 'problem', girls know why they walk away from these prestigious parts of the curriculum. They know there is a conflict between being a good girl and a good scientist. They know that boys do not ordinarily like 'girls who wear glasses' and who are good at maths and science. And when they know that girls are supposed to find fulfilment, self-realisation – even happiness – in pleasing boys, then the course of action to be taken is perfectly plain: it is to stay clear of science and mathematics.

Women 'withdraw' because their presence, and their competence, can detract from the performance and achievement of men. And society in general and men in particular have ways and means of pressurising and punishing women who will not take their proper propitiating place and help to protect an enhanced image of men. Girls in school who will not recognise the no-go areas are not in a pleasant position: they are generally neither popular nor protected.

Sometimes it is the boys in the classroom who put on the

pressure. Sometimes, however, it is the teacher who does the harassing, as many women are aware.

'My maths teacher would only teach the boys,' Deborah told us. 'If he wasn't ignoring the girls he was making some sort of sarcastic remark about why we shouldn't be there. You know, why would a girl want to know about algebra? He'd go on and on about how girls couldn't *do* mathematics. And he'd never ask a girl to answer a question. Anything you wanted to know you had to pick up for yourself. He really knew how to undermine your confidence.'

'We had this maths teacher who used to make a big thing out of the boys doing well,' said Annie. 'I wasn't bad at maths. Funny really, I quite liked maths. Didn't seem all that hard to get the answers – but you didn't let on, of course. Wasn't worth it. If I ever got the right answer before any of the boys, this old teacher would go right off the deep end. You know, all that stuff about what's the matter with you boys? – letting a girl beat you! He'd get tough with the boys and sure enough, they'd take it out on me. One boy twisted my arm once. Said he'd bloody break it if I did so well in the next test . . .'

How far had she gone with her mathematics education, we asked. Not far, was the reply. 'I kept it up for O level, but I'm not stupid. After that I failed.'

Another woman remembered her first science lesson because it had come as such a shock: 'It was my first time in the laboratory and I was really interested in all the equipment. I thought it was going to be great to get to do all those experiments. And then the teacher said he was pleased to see so many girls in the class because there would be such a lot of washing up to do. I thought he was joking, but he meant it. That's all we girls ever got to do – clean up.'

While the boys in her class did the experiments, she told us, the girls had to watch. Then while the boys wrote up the results the girls cleared up. 'Later I realised just what the teacher was doing,' she said angrily. 'He made all the girls helpless. He made them all dependent on the boys. Because when we wanted any notes in science – we had to go to the boys for them.'

While this woman was aware of the ways in which the superiority of men can be 'created' – and was angered by the injustice of the arrangement – it would be misleading to imply that all the women interviewed were equally resistant or rebellious when they recognised the significance of some of the educational practices to which they had been subjected. Some were resigned. When asked how they felt, some women simply shrugged their shoulders and said it was how the world worked, and women had better get used to it, and the sooner the better.

'It's no good getting upset,' one woman said philosophically, 'it's not going to change. *We* know men aren't really superior, that we are just pretending most of the time. But men don't, and that's the tricky bit. And we have to go on playing their game. So schools are just preparing girls for the real world.'

Whether schools should prepare pupils to perpetuate the status quo – prepare girls and boys to fit into the present system with its prescribed sex roles – or whether schools should actively promote change were questions for which women had a variety of answers. There was more consensus on the question of confidence, however: most women believed that a systematic attempt had been made within the school to undermine their confidence (and, interestingly, those who did *not*, without exception, came from single-sex schools). Some thought it was outrageous that the school should have eroded them in this way and some thought it a hard but necessary lesson that girls had to learn in order to be socialised for life. But all who had been to mixed-sex schools – and some who had been to single-sex schools – reported feeling that the school was instrumental in raising *self-doubt*, and that the same process was not applied to boys.

Women who were of the opinion that their confidence had been 'taken away' quoted a variety of examples to illustrate their point. Some said it was the overall atmosphere of the school where girls had been treated as second rate. Some gave as the cause a particular teacher – or teachers – who expected little of girls. Some said it was their experience in maths and science – they had been so regularly informed that girls could not 'do maths and science', that they had come to believe it. They lost their confidence and were no longer even willing to try.

Psychological studies are not required to demonstrate that people who are constantly informed that they cannot perform certain tasks are likely to begin to believe in their own incompetence, thereby helping to make the original assertion come true. They lose their confidence and doubt their ability: 'It's not just that we have to make men feel big, but that we have to feel small,' Deborah said.

Recent research corroborates the experience of these women (see Rosie Walden and Valerie Walkerdine, 1985; and Judith Whyte *et al*, 1985). Investigating mathematics ability – and anxiety – in girls, Sheila Tobias (1978) found that their level of confidence was dramatically lower than that of boys. This was revealed when girls and boys got the same grade in a mathematics test, but interpreted it very differently. The girl who got a high grade generally considered herself lucky, while the boy who got a high grade was more inclined to believe that he deserved it. The same mark, but the girl considered her ability was being *over*-rated while the boy thought it an accurate assessment of his. As far as Sheila Tobias was concerned it was the different level of confidence in the sexes which accounted for these different constructions placed upon the results. The difference also applied to low grades: the girl with the low grade thought that she had been 'found out' and her 'true' level of incompetence discovered. But the boy was more likely to see a bad grade as bad luck: next time he would do better.

Of course, mathematics is not the only area where girls have been taught to mistrust success – according to the girls, and to educational research. In her survey in primary schools Kathy Clarricoates (1978) found that girls were consistently better at some skills than boys – like reading and writing, for example – but that teachers did not *value* this achievement in girls. It was not taken as a sign of success. Rather teachers *expected* girls to be good at reading and writing and their achievement was therefore a non-event: it could be discounted.

And far from being rewarded for their efforts, the girls could actually be penalised. For when the girls performed better than the boys, teachers had good reason for spending more time with the boys. As Katherine Clarricoates observed, girls were placed in a 'no-win' situation in schools. It wasn't just in the scientific subjects that the teachers 'ignored' the girls: the reasons may have been reversed but the results were much the same in literary subjects where, once more, girls were overlooked. Again, they took second place as the bulk of the teachers' time went to the boys.

The effects of such treatment are not hard to find. Many women to whom we spoke knew from direct experience what Katherine Clarricoates and other researchers had found in their work: namely that when one is treated as unimportant, when one is ignored and overlooked, it takes its toll in self-esteem: 'At school the message was always that boys were better and brighter,' Deborah said with bitterness, 'and I believed I wasn't as good as a boy.'

Again and again women volunteered information on the way they had been taught to take second place to boys at school. We were told of how teachers of both sexes perceived the educational problems of boys as being more serious than the same problems when found in girls. We were told of how teachers of both sexes gave more encouragement and attention to the boys and how more excuses were made for boys when they were bad or below standard. We were told of how teachers of both sexes provided 'favourable' treatment for boys – even to the extent of giving them higher marks because they were boys.

'I used to make a fuss about handing in essays with our names on them,' Deborah said, 'because you just knew how she'd mark them. She thought boys were better – or should be better – and she always gave them better marks. If we could have had numbers – if the teacher hadn't known whose work she was marking – the girls would have done a lot better.' Research on 'blind' marking, from primary school tests to teacher-training reports and papers submitted for consideration to academic journals, suggests that there is substance to Deborah's assertion (see Dale Spender, 1984).

Not that all the women shared Deborah's ideas on the better performance of boys: some sincerely believed that boys did do better on average and that they genuinely *earned* the higher grades. 'When a boy puts his mind to it, he's generally better at it than a girl,' one woman said. To Deborah, admissions by women that men were 'better' said more about women's low self-esteem than about men's performance.

Whether or not the response was 'invited' most women wanted to speculate on how far teachers were responsible for giving girls lessons in subordination. That it was the *fault* of the teachers, and that schools and society would change if only teachers were to change, was the most commonly held view. But some women did not think it sensible to single out teachers to take all the blame: teachers were as much 'products of socialisation' as were women themselves. Two women teachers put forward this view.

'Teachers and students of both sexes think boys are more important,' said Heather, providing a theoretical explanation. 'It's

57

the social code. It's what society believes. That's why *all* the teachers can spend more time with the boys. It's why male *and* female teachers can take boys more seriously. And it turns into a self-fulfilling prophecy – so the boys really do become more important, they are *made* more important. Then the kids and the teachers, the girls and the boys think how right they were to start with the idea that boys are more important.'

More blunt and explicit was the second response: 'Teachers don't have any choice. Even if they didn't think boys were more important they'd have to behave as if they are. They have to plan their lessons for the boys, spend time with the boys, get the interest of the boys. Because if they don't – the boys riot. Schools don't just teach women to "reflect men", as you call it. They teach boys to get rough, if they don't get what they want,' Barbara told us.

Why schools and teachers do what they do is a matter for debate, and further research. But there is no great debate about *what* they do: what we heard was a depressingly long list of discriminatory attitudes and activities. Every woman who had ever been in a classroom with a male (school, college or university) could quote examples of harassment and 'teasing' and could comment on the impossibility of trying to make a complaint.

'When you asked for help against the boys at school you got about as much joy from most teachers as you get when you ask the police for help in cases of domestic violence – or rape,' said one woman, who went on to elaborate how girls could get the *blame* for the violent behaviour of boys. 'It's the ultimate insult to women,' she said, 'the ultimate test in organising society to suit men. When it's made women's fault that men are brutal. When women can be punished. When people say the woman should have managed it better.'

Another interviewee, Mona, was angry about the way she had been treated at school, and enraged by the way her daughter was being treated now. It was bad enough that as a child she had been unable to protect herself from the harassment of boys but it was outrageous, she thought, that as an adult she could not protect her own child from the same treatment.

'It's having to tie a boy's shoelaces today,' she said, 'but it will be having to do a man's dirty washing tomorrow. It's being told – by a four-year-old boy, mind you – that girls are stupid.

Tomorrow it will be that girls are only good for one thing.' And she listed all the unfair practices of the nursery school her daughter attended. She could do so quite readily because she had itemised them all in an open letter of protest that she had written to the teachers and parents when her 'discussions' at the school met with no positive response.

That even at four years of age the girls were required to wait on the boys, to serve them with orange juice and to clean up afterwards, was enough to incense Mona. That the boys had free run of the play facilities while the girls were confined to corners made her, in her words, 'hopping mad'. And that at such an early age the boys were insulting the girls, continually declaring that girls could not play ball, could not do certain puzzles, and were 'definitely dumb', filled her with frustration. Yet when she had tried to improve the educational climate for her daughter, the very values she was trying to alter were brought out and used against her.

'After the letter they set up a really formal meeting. And along came two loud daddies who'd never shown their faces before. Never seen them at anything that we'd organised for the children, or where there was any hard work to be done. But there they were, and did they hold the floor. It was a woman who chaired the meeting, and she called herself the chairman, and she let the two men do most of the talking. When I said she should call herself a chair*woman*, that this was another example of what I was complaining about – she just, well – she just went crazy. Every time I tried to say something she said I was being rude to the men. It was the two daddies who had come to sort everything out.'

Mona took her daughter out of nursery school. There was, she said, nothing else she could do. There was no way the school was going to change its practices and if anything she had only made it worse for her daughter by her intervention. For Mona it was another lesson in powerlessness.

Equally angered by the attitudes and activities of her daughter's school was Cathy, the mother of an adolescent girl who – according to Cathy – was daily being taught that the world was populated by only one sex. Cathy registered her various and vociferous objections to the secondary school curriculum which she gauged to be overwhelmingly and almost exclusively about men, men's needs and men's interests.

'And I know why it's all about men,' she said sarcastically.

'Because boys only want to hear about men. About great and good – and gory – men. They don't want to know about women. If you don't believe me,' she said, throwing down the challenge, 'just go into a classroom – a nursery school classroom or an Oxbridge classroom – and try and talk about women. Start talking about the things women are interested in and see how far you get. The men will go mad,' she said with certainty.

In Cathy's view it was the male students who directly and indirectly ensured that the substance of the curriculum was primarily 'male' by the simple expediency of 'kicking up a fuss' when it was not. 'In secondary school they will say it's "sissy" to have to learn about women and women's interests. In the university they'll say it lowers the standard. Either way, you end up with a curriculum based on the interests and feats of men,' she said.

This was how males became the centre of the classroom and the centre of the curriculum as far as Cathy was concerned. This was how females were taught that they were only entitled to second place. Because for generations girls have been reared on *woman-less history* (as the writer Rebecca West so aptly put it); and it is not because women do not have a history every bit as illuminating and exciting as men's. It is because males do not want to hear about women's glorious past: it 'takes away' from the primacy of their own. Or at least this is the explanation provided by some women, some teachers and some educational researchers.

'History and literature as they are taught in school are full of stories about drama and danger on the eve of battle – when men are about to risk death and think a lot about the meaning of life. But men have never been alone in facing death, or risking death. Women have done it too,' Deborah explained. 'But you won't find anything about the dangers that millions of women have faced on the eve of childbirth. You won't find out in the classroom about the courage, the pain – and the absence of choice – for ordinary women who have risked death by *giving* life. That's not in the curriculum. And don't tell me it's because it's not interesting, not dramatic – not sufficiently significant. It's because it doesn't add to the great image of men.'

From a survey of the educational curriculum it would be reasonable to conclude that the deeds of men are held up for praise while those of women are overlooked. It would be reasonable to conclude that the feats of great men are emphasised –

which is how they get to be great men – while those of women are rendered invisible – which is why there are so few great women. And it would be reasonable to conclude that the picture of society, the sexes, and their achievements, which is portrayed within learning materials, is not an accurate one: rather it is a distorted picture in which the image of one sex is 'blown up' while that of the other is 'reduced' (see Marion Scott, 1980 and Judith Whyte *et al*, 1985).

For those who learn to make sense of the world on the basis of what they have been taught, the curriculum is a significant source of information: it conveys the message that boys are more important and that girls are to take second place. This is the conclusion of an increasing number of educational researchers.*

That they are 'less worthy' is also the conclusion of most women students. Being 'good' students can mean they learn quickly to take second place to men. They can learn – in school and university – that it is desirable and necessary for women to 'hold back', to conceal their capabilities and to develop dependence: they can learn that they are required to stay in the wings so that men can have sole and unchallenged occupancy of the centre stage.

This is how women are undermined: it is how the problem of doubting their own abilities is compounded as they start to deny their own psychological and intellectual resources and begin to augment those of men. There was no woman to whom we spoke who did not quote some experience of being obliged to bolster the ego and the intellectual achievement of men. The basic area of difference was the extent to which they resented having to undertake this chore.

It was the women who had the most education who were most vociferous in their complaints of having to hide their own abilities to enhance those of men. We talked with Carey, now a Fellow at a Cambridge College, who itemised all the problems a clever woman must contend with. To illustrate her case she quoted Jane Austen, who had written that 'A woman, especially if she should have the misfortune of knowing anything, should conceal it as well as she can.'

As far as Carey was concerned, little progress had been made in the more than one hundred and fifty years since those words had

* The same conclusion has been reached in relation to issues of race and class.

61

been written. And she told us of all the self-effacing tactics that bright women found they had to use in the company of men, the men they worked with and the men they lived with.

Carey talked about the double standard, how the world had stopped when her husband had been doing his Ph.D. (and how it had been her job to stop it), but how little help – or even encouragement – she had received from him when she was doing the research for her own Ph.D.

Carey also revealed – perhaps unknowingly – that the lessons she had learnt about the lesser importance of girls had taken their toll on her own confidence and self-esteem. 'All the games bright girls have to play to pretend they aren't bright, to prove they're not a threat,' she said, 'and in my case it's all such a waste because I'm not bright at all.' A Doctor of Philosophy? A Fellow of a Cambridge College? A doubter of her own abilities! This is one of the aspects of anxiety about success among women which has attracted the attention of researchers like Matina Horner and Sheila Tobias.

Less research attention has been given to the documentation of the daily duties demanded of women who work with men. Yet this 'petty boosting' is known to all women in this situation and is usually irritatingly difficult to bear. Helen, a lecturer in teacher education made this very clear when she gave one example after another of the way she and her women colleagues were obliged to 'look after' the men on the staff. The women, she said, constantly managed the men, partly by camouflaging their own capabilities, partly by providing ready and repeated reassurances to the men. It was just easier in the long run, she confessed, to let the men look more knowledgeable and more important. But she didn't feel good about what she was doing: she thought it was bad for the staff and bad for the students.

'It's got nothing to do with numbers,' she said. 'You don't have to have a room full of men to get the women to look after them. Sometimes you only need one man. In fact, one man can get the support of just about every woman in the room. We've got plenty of courses where there are more women than men on them, but the women still defer to the men. They see the staff doing it; they do it; the kids they teach do it. There's no end to it.'

Laura, an arts lecturer, agreed. 'We spend so much time protecting the men, it's a wonder we have any time left to do research,' she said. 'Academic males' egos are so fragile. They just fall apart unless women rush round after them. They're so pathetic – and we're so pathetic because we just keep coming to the rescue all the time. We make all the soothing noises and then it works against us when we want to say something serious and to be seen as professional colleagues.

'Not that it stops them using our ideas though,' she said sagely and went on to describe a situation which is familiar to many women.

"THAT'S AN EXCELLENT SUGGESTION, MS WINTHROP. WE'LL WAIT FOR ONE OF THE MEN HERE TO MAKE IT."

'A woman makes a suggestion at a meeting, and it's like she hasn't spoken. Doesn't even make a ripple in the conversation. Fifty seconds later a man says the *same* thing – and it's suddenly a good idea! It happens all the time. And if you ask the men why they took no notice of the woman's suggestion, they'll swear they didn't hear it. Or they'll insist she didn't say it. And that's one way men get to look as though they have *all* the ideas.

Some of the situations described had their humorous elements but some were far more serious. Among the most distressing accounts of women's subordination and exploitation was that given by Lesley, a mature college student, who described the behaviour of some of the male staff to the young female students. 'They can deny it all they like,' she insisted, 'but what's going on is that some women are getting the message that they'll do better on their course if they hand out sexual favours. And a lot of these young women don't have the confidence to think they can make it on their own – or the confidence to challenge some of these pricks who call themselves educators – so they go along with it. They could be right of course. It might be the only way for women to pass the course. I wouldn't put it past a few of those bastards to fail any women they thought were being nasty to them. And I tell you, they can even think that a women who doesn't smile at them is being nasty to them. It's just so much better for their bloody egos to have all these attractive young women falling all over them.'

Lesley's vituperation, however, was not reserved solely for the male staff. She had a few words to say on the topic of young women who felt flattered by the sexual attentions of their tutors: 'While women continue to *like* being sex objects, and to like being *treated* as sex objects, it makes it even harder to change men,' she said somewhat wearily.

But if the women we interviewed had some depressing tales to tell about their own past and present, what is probably even more disturbing is that it appears that the education system which 'put them down' is doing much the same to their daughters, despite the belief in progress and despite the rhetoric of equal educational opportunity.

From our interviews it appears appropriate to conclude that girls in school now are, in substance, learning the same lessons that their mothers and grandmothers learnt before: the lessons of subordination. They are learning to hide their skills so men may look superior. They are learning to project and promote a positively inflated image of man.

And they are doing precisely what Cicely Hamilton described more than seven decades ago. They are fostering the fallacy that women are inferior to men. And this is a source of petty hindrance to them. But what women would be like if they were to stop is still a matter for guesswork. What women would be like if free to bloom rather than obliged to remain in the shade is as much a matter of speculation for the present generation as it was for Cicely Hamilton's. While education continues to indoctrinate and constrain as it does, we cannot know what women could be.

4

THE FIGURE AND THE FACTS

There is substantial evidence that men's views on our bodies are more important than our own. Painted faces, shaved hair, uplifted breasts, blue-tacked smiles, stiletto heels . . . all these are body falsehoods which women invoke in the great male protection racket. Women are willing to perpetrate these lies to make men look taller, seem stronger, feel more powerful. Women have always lied with their bodies, to gain approval, because they've been led to believe that their own truths are not good enough for men's eyes. Men want us to be what they imagine, or fantasise, we are. They want us to be what they need. Something made-up. (That phrase itself is significant.) Something toned down. Something plastic, perfect, commercial and idealised. A sex object they can define, desire and control. Should our real, diverse and wobbly female flab not fit into these man-made prescriptions, there are many ways men can put women down.

So how do we act? We go out with a short man. We wear flat shoes. He looks taller. Feels bigger. We go out with a tall man. We trip in high heels. Look frail. He feels stronger. We don't go out with men. Wear clumpy, comfy shoes to please ourselves. Men jeer. We feel unfashionable. Having recognised this is something most women including ourselves do, we found we had come up with another contradiction. In order to please men, women wear flatties thereby losing height and any chance of looking superior. However, men seem even more delighted when women totter at their sides in high heels.

The woman in stilettos not only looks unsafe. She often *is* unsafe, as recent evidence shows a high correlation between the type of female footwear and the incidence of male attack. High heels are in a very real sense 'rape shoes'. Women who wear trainers or running shoes are actually less likely to be physically attacked, but more likely to attract male derision. Listen to Sonia, a stylist in a Cambridge unisex hair salon:

'If I'm a bit late for work, I get dressed up in my skinfits and tight wool shirt, but I shove my stilettos in a placcy bag and put on joggers so I can run there. No hassle till I reach the street the salon's on. Pretty fashionable down that way. So I get terrible comments from blokes right along the road. "Couldn't you keep the struggle up as far as your big flat pancakes?" one yelled yesterday. 'Got corns today pussy?' was another remark. Then there's the old standby: "What's a popsie like you doing with dykie shoes on?" '

Sonia says it makes her very upset and by the time she reaches the salon she is so embarrassed she rushes to change her shoes at once. 'It's stupid because I'm on my feet all day and after a few hours in heels I'm crippled!' One day she decided to be sensible and stay in her trainers. 'There were nasty comments from everyone, staff and clients. The most usual was "What's up Sonia, you're usually so fashion conscious? Got yourself a teeny weenie boyfriend?" '

Not one of Sonia's customers or any of her colleagues could credit she might have made the change for her own benefit. For both women and men believe that any choice women make about clothes or appearance must be a selection based on male interests. Why should it matter who looks taller? Why should it matter considerably more to men?

Nancy Henley, in a book called *Body Politics* (1977), gives us a clue. She says that the way we sit, smile, stare, cock our heads, take up space, or touch other people shows where we are in power relationships. Thus the ways in which women alter appearances by adjusting the height of their shoes, for example, play an important role in maintaining the social order and showing women's place within it. These non-verbal cues can be seen as signs of submission, symbols of dominance or even as subtle messages of threat.

How *do* women walk? Or, for that matter, how do they stand or sit? Do we show dominance or deference by our posture? Henley discovered that women avert their eyes more than men do; frequently, they hunch down and drop their gaze when men stare at them. This is what sociological researchers describe as habitually submissive behaviour.

What about the stance known as 'military bearing', an example of the appearance of command? That is almost always male. According to Henley, standing tall is a good way of achieving dominance. As in our culture more tall people are men, those men who are short have a very good reason for wanting to appear taller (p.89).

Reading this research on height and power made us realise that the way women stand and hold themselves publicly can show men whether the women consider themselves as victims or whether they feel firmly self-assertive. Being treated as 'street wise' and therefore not available for sexual harassment can often be a matter of the signals given out by women's body posture.

All our interviewees agreed that many women they knew wore flat-heeled shoes to please their boyfriends who wanted to appear taller but not one of them admitted to having done it themselves. Either they all had tall boyfriends or they all told tall stories!

We can, however, write from firsthand experience about our own wedding days (three between the two authors) and explain why one of us wore flatties (which was playing the game properly) and both of us caused consternation amongst the wedding guests by speaking up instead of shutting up (which was playing the game highly improperly). Sally had a particular problem at her first wedding.

My first husband was two inches shorter than I was. My mother suggested I wore flat-heeled shoes. 'He is the groom, darling. The man of the moment. This is to be the most memorable occasion in both your lives. You must look your best for it.'

But looking our best meant very different things to each of us. To look his best, the groom wore black tails and a *top hat* (to add a few more inches?). To look my best, I had planned to wear bright scarlet or purple and very high heels. (I am not tall either and wanted to look more confident.) The family were aghast. 'Darling,' Mother said, 'it's quite out of the question. Brides never stand out, not in *that* way.'

At the time, I didn't think Mother and Jilly Cooper had much in common, but later reading Jilly Cooper's book *How to Stay Married* (1969), I realised that on the subject of weddings and men, their advice is remarkably similar. Cooper has three admonitions for brides: The first is 'Be careful what you wear, look pretty but not outrageous' (p.50). The second is 'Don't forget to take the price tags off your new shoes, they'll show when you kneel down in church' (p.11). The third is 'Brides, don't be disappointed if you don't look your best, far more likely you'll be scarlet in the face and piggy-eyed from lack of sleep' (p.11).

"Do you promise to reflect this man?"

Under pressure, I did in fact look something like Jilly Cooper and mother's model bride. I gave up the idea of scarlet or purple, wore white lace, a fixed smile and extremely *low* white satin shoes with no visible price tag. Come to think of it there were no visible price tags anywhere on my body, but I think I knew I'd been bought. I'd sold out to a system which has huge receptions, labelled mothers' memorable occasions in which mothers' daughters painstakingly reflect other mothers' sons.

Why do women do it? In my case I think it was my old enemy, an anxiety to please. Because of our anxiety to please, women are constantly distracted from what they want to do. On that first wedding day, my husband had carefully prepared his speech. I had carefully prepared a speech too. There was another family uproar. Father said my clever young husband was an articulate journalist, a good debater and an expert in after-dinner speaking. He would make an appropriate speech in the proper manner. Father said that my role was to look demure ('please, for once try to *smile* rather than to speak') and bask in my new husband's attentions. There was to be *no* question of my making a speech. It simply wasn't done. Father reminded me that, *at last* (and unless something dreadful occurred), I was about to become a wife. Wives, Mother inserted, do not speak on such occasions, or if they do they are not heard unless what they are saying flatters their husbands. Mother had years of experience to draw upon. My husband, however, was an unusually understanding man. A kind and considerate person, he found my eccentricities amusing and my outspokenness attractive. He wanted the occasion to be good for me too and was prepared to humour me. He persuaded my father to *let me* speak. I was allowed to say a few words before my husband's 'real' speech. I had no right to speak at my own wedding. I only spoke with the consent of the men in my life. I was allowed to be special and different; of course, my speech reflected my new husband's liberality and kindness. How could it not?

I wondered if I was a rare species of womankind but, to my relief, I discovered that Dale had spoken at her wedding too, and had caused equal consternation. In her case, her speech was unplanned and unprepared. Most of the guests immediately labelled her domineering and her husband produced expressions of 'deep regret' for his new wife's extraordinary behaviour.

On my second wedding day, the issue was even more clear cut. It was a large public affair. I am ashamed to admit that the reception was held at London's Playboy Club with the bunny girls in attendance. My second husband was a public figure who commanded attention. I was just the ex-journalist who had once interviewed him. This time both our speeches were ready. The reporters didn't ask me a single question. I remembered Father's advice and smiled grimly. This time I had decided to wear whatever *I* chose. No boring white lace dress nor subservient flatties, but an outrageous orange leather trouser suit with tall black boots. Mother appeared at the wedding dressed in black. Would it get reported that her daughter wore *orange*? Oh, the shame of that outfit. She needn't have worried. Every newspaper report was headed 'Purple trousers for bridegroom' or 'Musician wears stunning purple and black regency gear'.

Thinking back to what now seems to have been my bizarre playgirl era, I recall that at around the same time, reporter Gloria Steinem successfully completed an assignment to be a bunny girl, in which she was taught every pleasing means to 'make it seem that the (male) customer's opinions are very important' (p.40). Twenty years later, in 1983, she wrote that she realised that 'all women are bunnies' (p.69).

Acceptable body language, like appropriate conversation, is the kind that offers deference. As Edith Wharton reputedly said, 'Genius is of small use to a woman who does not know how to do her hair' (1900, p.338). Women learn to do their hair or do away with their hair (under the arms, around the pubis) in the ways and places men wish us to. John Ruskin had only seen idealised versions of naked women before he married; conventional wisdom has it that, seeing his wife's pubic hair, he was so revolted that he was unable to consummate the marriage. Apparently, men like Ruskin are still about.

Women we talked to all encountered men with body hair phobias, some in the privacy of the bedroom, others in public hospital wards. This is Fiona's story: 'I was going into hospital to have a sterilisation done. I checked before I went with a gynaecologist. Did I have to have a pubic shave? "Absolutely not," she said. But minutes after admission, I was confronted by a nurse, "scythe" in hand. After a long argument, she agreed the shave wasn't necessary for the operation *but it was for the doctor*. "He won't operate if you don't have it shaved," she said. "Mr Morrell doesn't like hairy women. He insists we do it." ' It was within Fiona's right to refuse. But when the nurses told her if she did she might as well go straight home, she allowed her pubic hair to be shaved off.

In *Man Made Language*, Dale pointed out that not only does hair have to be removed but the *signs of removal must be removed*. Dale's own ex-husband had a fit if he saw her razor lying about because it made it clear that she actually did grow hair (just as he did) and it was hair that *had to be removed*. He wanted desperately to think hair did not exist under the arms of any woman but most particularly not under the arms of the one he had chosen to marry.

Do women shave away hair because subconsciously they know men want them to appear not only young but also immature? Even older women are required to razor off rubble in order to produce a facsimile of the lean, smooth, sexually immature girls they once were; a hairfree sexual image that connotes *powerlessness*.

Certainly the 1980s shape is one reminiscent of adolescence. Although there has been an increase in the earnings of young people, which would encourage the fashion industry to bear that in mind, it isn't the main reason why today's fashionable figure is an immature body. The ideal, interestingly enough, is not a young girl but an older woman who has retained her adolescent figure. This valuation of immaturity is on the lines of the more prepubescent we are, the more likely we may be to value and reflect the powerful male sex.

Not only what we shave off but also what we put on is of great significance. Throughout history, women have crippled, restricted and moderated their bodies' natural movements to what they have been told is an acceptable style. Body images illustrate that most women are prepared to be less than they could be. Few have the strength and determination of director/actress Mae West (1984) who in an interview said that if any man wanted her to diminish herself, she could get on easily without him. The independent and wealthy (this latter fact having a certain significance) Ms West, who confessed she had been in more laps than a napkin, spoke of the pressure she had encountered to reflect men physically. She said that when a man was courting her, he'd want to put a diamond on her finger and as soon as he thought he had her, he wanted to put an apron round her waist. She didn't want any diamond handcuffs. She had her career to think about and any man who wanted her to be less than she was, she didn't need.

Though all our interviewees had somewhat more mundane handcuffs than Ms West, many shared her resentment. This is what Nan told us: 'It all comes down to bodies! Men want us to look like they do in Mayfair. If your body doesn't come up to scratch, you've had it. Blokes like women who look like my friend Christine. It costs her a fortune. Loads of make-up and beautiful willowy clothes that slink. She even dresses up to stay in with her husband. Every time I see her I think, "I must buy something that slinks, and wear it with red stilettos like she does." It's ridiculous as I've got short, fat, hairy legs and you can't trudge round a laboratory in something slinky!'

Nan's friend Christine has obviously taken to heart Jilly Cooper's injunction that no wife has any right to let herself go to seed after she's married (p.56). This idea of slackening up implies that the behaviour needed to win approval is very hard work. 'If you want to keep your husband you'll have to work hard to go on attracting him' (p.57).

We found that even women who don't work at it are envious of the effects of those who do. Kim, a thirty-five-year-old primary school teacher at a village school told us how envious, and alarmed, she had been when she first met her colleagues. 'Most of the women were younger than I was. Very skinny, more like models than teachers. They wear trendy size-ten clothes and flatter and dance attention on the Head, a middle-aged powerful man who basks in their admiration. I'm a hefty fourteen. I feel like a painstaking elephant teaching the kids. Whilst avoiding confrontation with the boss, and worrying about not getting promotion, I can't imagine why he hired me except I had very good references and qualifications. I just wish he'd treat the women staff like he does the men. As long as they work well they can be fat or slop around in jeans.'

Bored with these unnatural efforts, some women had experimented with not wearing make-up. Few found the male responses easy to bear. Annabel who works in a chemist said her boss told her it was disgusting not to wear cosmetics in her trade, apart from the fact that she looked frightful without make-up! Dale says she can remember the first time she stopped wearing cosmetics and how peculiar it felt. 'It was very frightening, though in retrospect it's hard to believe just how traumatising it was. The moment I stopped everyone noticed. Some of my colleagues interpreted it as a hostile act. Several of them said, "So we are not worth bothering about any more, eh?" Others made petty comments about how I looked older and they could see very well why make-up was necessary for a woman like me.'

Jennifer, who works in an opticians', said: 'I'd like to give up but I'm frightened of bad comments. Eyes . . . that's my weakness. I always feel men who come in for new spectacles will be watching my eyes. They want me to look like the mascara-ed women on the shop posters. One chap said, "Girls like you, with those awful pale lashes, ought to sleep in mascara." You don't forget a remark like that!'

Pearl, a local radio producer, said that her problem was the contrast between her fragile appearance and her strong character. 'Because I look the little woman image, I fell into wearing frail fabrics and pastels and big soulful blue-shadowed eyes. So the men at work treat me like a fairy doll then get tight-lipped with fury when they find I'm hard as hell professionally. It's as if I've cheated them out of their dues. I'd like to change my fashion image but I will find it hard to give up mascara and eyeliner.'

It is no accident that women like Jennifer and Pearl try to retain eye make-up. Some key sociological studies point out that eyes and eye contact have particular importance in women's lives. It is interesting to speculate what women think of the very few men who attempt to flutter wistfully or gaze soulfully!

Research tells us that women engage in more eye contact than men; that it is women who do most of the looking, particularly when men are speaking; and that more eye contact is characteristic of those who seek approval from others. Annie, a married secondary school teacher, adds her view to the findings. 'It's not enough for me to listen to my husband while I mark the kids' homework. He always wants me to drop everything, even their school books, and make sure my eyes are on him while he's talking. He frequently says "Annie you're not looking at me!" '

When the authors were very young women, there were some amusing etiquette books which prescribed dropping the eyes as proper facial behaviour for modest young ladies. Today, it is more often fear of violence which encourages women, of all ages, to drop their eyes when they encounter men in the streets. If men want to know what it is like to be a woman, they should try this exercise which Nancy Henley quotes in her book *Body Politics*.

'Walk down a city street . . . Look straight ahead . . . Every time a man walks past you, avert your eyes and make your face expressionless. Most women learn to go through this act each time we leave our houses. It's a way to avoid at least some of the encounters we've all had with strange men who decided we looked available' (p.164).

Women seldom question the way all men stare at them, yet this is a constant feature of their lives. Women are taught early to put up with this barrage of rudeness, even told it is complimentary.

'An Italian who makes eyes at you is simply being polite,' says

Geneviève Dariaux. And she describes an Englishman as: 'The gentleman who obviously has eyes only for your lips and bosom as you talk and you say to yourself, "I see what he's after . . . there's no point in my trying to be witty" ' (p.351).

Women's clothes, usually designed by men, also diminish and impede women's gestures, abilities and natural tastes. Many women have willingly consented to fashionable imprisonment within straight skirts that restrict, corsets that clutch and girdles that grasp. How little that says for our self-respect.

A few years ago, to be fashionable meant to conform to a tight rather than loose prevailing sexual ideal. Fashion photographs showed women tightly encased with figure-hugging contour lines. This circumspection, this tightness of demeanour (which researchers like Goffman and Henley emphasise are usually those of status inferiors) displayed in women's clothes, also showed up in the tension of their bodies. Studies found that females were generally less relaxed than males and conveyed a more submissive attitude through tenser postures (Goffman, 1963, p.12).

Conversely, stereotypes suggest that a 'loose woman' (often portrayed as much by her clothes and body posture as by temperament) is one of bad reputation and her so-called looseness comes from lack of accepted control over her sexuality. It is interesting that portrayals in fiction or drama often carry with them displays of looseness in clothing and posture. An excellent example was Anna Magnani, the Italian actress who created just such a 'loose' character in *The Rose Tattoo* and in *Open City*.

The way that men define women's clothes (or bodies) and thereby their characters is part of a Catch 22 syndrome where no matter what a woman does, she can't get it right. Take the loose-tight sequence. Just as the loose woman is condemned for sexual permissiveness, so is the tight woman who doesn't relax enough and is condemned for being a prude. These opposing demands are not, however, as contradictory as they seem, for they fit into the traditional male view that a woman must restrict her sexuality (and its symbols) to all but one person (usually male) with whom she has a sacred relationship and for whom she is supposed to be an endlessly flowing fountain of effervescent passion.

Not content with designing clothes to obstruct and frustrate the natural woman, men have also invented *accessories*. How many men either need or use a handbag? Male design of women's clothes has largely precluded pockets. This means that women are forced to carry purses, to shoulder satchels, to lug handbags. Have you ever tried running down a platform to catch a train just about to move off, whilst pushing a baby in a buggy, hanging on to three parcels in one hand, clutching your purse and grabbing your slipping shoulder-bag and two wriggling toddlers with the other hand? If you do make it to the train, the next problem is how and with what do you open the door?

'The function of the purse as women's albatross makes it a symbol of ridicule' (Nancy Henley, p.90). Quite so! It is little wonder that unpleasant impersonations of male homosexuals also use a handbag as a mark of shame. Who wants to look like a woman?

Posture itself is part of the training that shackles women into 'feminine' roles. It emphasises propriety. Keep the legs closed when sitting down. Don't lean over so that breasts escape. Keep the skirt pulled to the shifting fashionable leg level. If there's a hint of trouble, cross your legs fast! With such restrictions on demeanour, dress and shape, it is noticeable which women try to reflect men physically and which do not. Joan Cassell (1977) observes that differences between groups of women can be spotted by their deportment, clothes or bearing. Two strikingly different groups were those who belonged to the Women's Liberation Movement and those who did not.

'The more radical the ideology the more recognizable the demeanour' (p.83). She observed that those who reflected men the least were radical lesbian feminists who were unlikely to wear conventionally stereotyped tight clothes, and were often discovered in comfortable jeans or baggy overalls that hid the wearer's shape. These women, she observed, also behaved in a non-admiring way to men. They talked back to street hecklers, carried heavy loads with pride, changed their own tyres, repaired and operated their own public address systems. Women who wear trousers or ties to suit themselves are illustrating an admirable, authentic autonomy. But today male designers are encouraging fashionable women to adopt male-style suits in order to win male approval.

The butch suit, or the bib-and-braces outfit, originally borrowed by radical women who wanted both to dissociate themselves from feminine stereotypes and claim an active sexual identity, today is sold even in chain stores like Marks & Spencer.

" I'LL COME STRAIGHT TO THE POINT, MISS WILSON.
I DON'T LIKE YOUR ATTITUDE."

The designers do not suppress the original meanings; they use hints of them to add a provocative touch of allure. 'The slight suggestion of lesbianism is taken as an extreme point of daring,' observes Rosalind Coward (p.35). However, these clothes have nothing to do with the real daring of attempting to love one's own sex and thereby implicitly not to reflect men ... but only to do with daring for the attention of *men*.

'This fashionable look ... the over-big, often ill-fitting suit and tie – is a statement about daring not to seek the approval of men but presenting yourself in a way so that you know you'll get it. I don't have to seek after male approval (but I'm damn sure I'll get it because men like women who'll do anything)' (p.35). Once again, this is an example of the appearance of a male ideology which reinforced women's passivity. Clothes symbolise both sexual deference and feminine appreciation. If this is returned at all by men, it will be in terms of men's competence, protectiveness and admiration but only for women's negative qualities. Underlying this exchange is an implicit division of areas of competence into 'masculine' and 'feminine'. The real exchange that goes on under the term sexual deference is women deferring to men but not the reverse, and men patronising women for deferring to them.

As long as this exchange continues those areas of competence will remain. Women will still be constrained to look up to men. Men will feel perfectly free to put women down. Even when they are wearing the appropriate clothes, and they have slimmed down to the right size, they still sometimes get put down – for doing just that. The nearer they edge physically to the perfect sexual ideal, the less seriously they are treated by men. In many professions, for instance, being skinny equals being sexy which equals being an incompetent worker.

Take the case of Dr Caroline Standlake, a social anthropologist at a major British university, who was asked to take over the presentation of a television series on different cultures. She lost a lot of weight, emerged suddenly with a striking slim figure and wore highly flamboyant, tight-fitting sweaters. The local newspaper suggested viewers watch the programme 'as much to see Caroline's latest trendy jumper as to learn about other societies!' (Caroline, please note, not Dr Standlake). One of her male colleagues told us: 'She used to be highly respected, but now she's called the Thinking Man's Crumpet and her work is being devalued.'

Our bodies may be ourselves but we do not yet control them. Our body language still exposes male ideas. Our body coverings are still being manipulated for male use. Most of all, our body size and weight is still the yardstick by which men measure us. And because of that, it also becomes the instrument by which we measure ourselves.

Sally, a long-suffering expert in the ways in which women reflect men physically, feels her own confession on this subject is long overdue.

'The crunch came at Christmas. Two women friends gave me an amazing and exotic . . . but desperately *public* beautify-the-body present. Now we all know that only women with already beautiful bodies can afford an open invitation to go on beautifying publicly. Everyone else is just that tiny bit hesitant about showing off their shape.

'What was it, this generous gift which made my soul shrink with trepidation and shyness? It was a full day's admission ticket to the Sanctuary, a most original ladies' health club in London. The ticket entitled me to spend from 10am to 10pm sweating it off, toning it up, taking it apart and rubbing it down ("it" being my not-so-beautiful body) in a club described in the brochure as having a unique swimming pool surrounded by tropical water garden complete with exotic birds and fabulous fish. All very wonderful. Around it are placed gentle jacuzzis, splendid saunas, double-sized sunbeds, vanity areas and herbal baths. All highly relaxing. There are fruit juice fountains, a health food bar, free magazines. What more could a hedonistic, full-figured feminist desire?

'But here's the catch. The brochure says: as the Sanctuary is reserved for ladies only, *swimwear is optional*!

'Optional? You mean *spend twelve hours publicly with NO CLOTHES ON*? Expose the figure – all of it – to the eyes of hundreds of strangers? All of them size-ten sylphs, no doubt! Impossible! My figure is only exposed under the most private conditions, to the most intimate of friends, either in semi-darkness or in the heat of passion or after a great deal of red wine (which is sometimes the same thing), preferably with someone who I am totally sure cares desperately deeply for my soul, has an underlying respect for my mind and couldn't think badly of my body if they were paid to.

'If you are a woman whose measurements are 34-24-36, all this may amuse you in a smirky sort of way but you cannot truly empathise. Every other woman will understand.

'Why didn't I throw my sacred Sanctuary admission ticket back in my kind friends' smiling faces? Firstly, I was stopped by the sheer lunatic expense of the gift. Secondly, by my friends' assurances that at least there would be *no men* gathered in the health club also optionally wearing (or heaven forbid *not* wearing) their swimsuits. That, I granted them, was a big relief.

'But why? Why is the presence of men near the naked female body so unnerving? I left them all discussing my humorous predicament, and sneakily went and got undressed and stood naked and slightly bulgy in front of a full-length mirror. Not a pose I can often be found in. But it was an excellent one for revelations relevant to this book. Basically, there wasn't a lot wrong with my figure by Botticelli's standards or Rubens's. What was drastically wrong was that neither the body nor the face in any way matches up to contemporary male standards of femininity.

'The face wasn't made up. The boobs weren't uplifted. The waist wasn't squeezed in. Indeed, there were several folds that fell out on either side of it. I cheered up when I looked a little lower. The legs were really quite trim. Then I remembered that when fully clothed they were usually in faded jeans cut off by flat-heeled boots. Not a great deal for men to approve of.

'Looking at the mirror, it became obvious that I ate, drank (possibly too much) and dressed to please myself. In that case, what are all these leftover hang-ups I still have about my body? These inhibitions are markedly similar to those many women have about their bodies, the most pervasive of which is related to weight.

'The worst thing you can be as a woman is FAT. Not because you are a danger to others. Not even primarily because you might be a danger to yourself. But because men won't like you. And if it is a woman's purpose in life to be liked by men then to be fat is to forego one of life's essential ingredients. It is to fail to meet the mark of male approval and acceptance.'

In general women deemed to be overweight are seen to be at fault. They have no discipline. They are out of control. How often does 'fat' get linked to 'slovenly'? Their size becomes a sign of their character.

Most women who are overweight do not like the state. They frequently feel the same contempt for themselves that society expresses towards them. There is such a taboo on female fatness in a society where women's task is to please men, that one of the hardest things for a woman to do is to admit that is what she is. The phrase that women find almost impossible to say is, 'I am fat'.

'I'm still not comfortable with the word,' Angie, a thirty-one-year-old trainee printer, told us. She was sure she had come to terms with her own body size, that she no longer went through the anguish she had experienced when she was younger. 'But I still find it very hard to admit that I'm not well, um, not thin. I just can't seem to easily say "Um I'm fat". It seems to imply such awful things about me. Saying that word makes me feel ashamed.'

Angie weighs about ten stone, is 5'3", looks very fit and rosy but still tends to huddle her body shape inside dark fishermen's smocks. 'I used to starve myself to get down to the eight-stone level when men would start fancying me. But it never suited me. I looked ill, felt miserable, so I'd go on a doughnut and cream-cake binge and up it would fly again. Today, I've taken up squash, eat less, and am more comfortable with my weight. But I still talk about my weight in comparative terms. I say "I'm heavier than I was last month" or "I'm thinner now I've taken up squash." '

Why is this? Why is women's worth measured in pounds? The less the number of pounds, the greater the worth of the woman.

Because thinness is so intertwined with male approval, it has been suggested in recent years that women who are fat might be registering a protest. Fat can be seen as a wilful rejection of male approval. Susie Orbach, author of *Fat Is A Feminist Issue* (1978), certainly thinks so. She says that 'being overweight is seen as deviance and anti-men' (p.17) and points out that because men control the normative goals offered to women, physical fitness, beauty and slimness have become major female pre-occupations.

Inevitably, the explanations offered for fatness point the finger of failure at the women themselves. Fat women are accused of: failing to control their weight; failing to control their appetites; failing to control their impulses; it is no wonder that fat women are often seen simply as failures! Over-eating and obesity, expressions of painful and conflicting experiences, are reduced to character defects simply because they do not reflect male values.

In our language, the word 'fat' is not neutral. It has strong derogatory connotations. This means it can effectively be used by men to put women down and hold them in line. We decided to ask women how this worked in practice.

Lucy, who works in a jam factory, is tall but has (in her opinion) breasts that are 'far too big' and a 'definite bulgy middle'. She has been a regular attender at her local Weight-Watchers for several years.

'But I've never told Ted, my bloke, that I was going, because that would have made him realise all his jibes about me being a "fattie" had "gotten to me". I didn't want him to know how much I minded.

'It was worse last summer. We went on a package holiday to Spain. If I refused to go down to the beach in a bikini, Ted would say, "Come on Lu, let it all hang out, what's a big bulge or two between old mates like us?" Then, if I gave in to his teasing and put on my bikini, he'd start wolf-whistling and shout to our group of friends: "Here she comes: larger than life Lulu! Roll up!

Roll up! The Biggest Show on Earth's about to start! What's not on show can't be that vital! Come and see for yourselves!'' Then, of course, they'd all have a good laugh. He never meant to be unkind but I spent most of that holiday in tears.'

We asked the other women in Lucy's group at Weight-Watchers whether they felt Ted was unusual. Sharon said decisively: 'I reckon they're all like that. My boyfriends were just the same. If you didn't look like some model, they'd wind you up by using words like podgy or bulgy. In the end, of course, I had to go to Weight-Watchers. There was nothing else I could do.'

Many of the women in Sharon and Lucy's group had either been sent there openly with their men's approval and backing or had been driven there secretly by despair at not getting approval. Most of the group had failed at calorie counts, miracle diets, and sheer brute willpower. Being a member of a fat women's collective was their last hope.

The next place we visited was a large gymnasium, where women go for lunchtime classes, trapped by the new 'slim for health' image.

Janice told us how she came to join a gym. 'I was staying in a youth hostel on a cycling holiday with three of my mates. It was the first time I'd been on holiday with other women. I didn't feel shy sharing a dormitory, not like you do with blokes. But they all three noticed that when I dressed or undressed and got to the bra stage, I'd turn away from them. One of them said in a friendly way: "Is it because we don't wear bras and you do? We're quite used to dangling boobs!" I tried to explain that whenever I've shared a room with a boyfriend, and had to take off my bra, I'd suck in my breath, draw in my flesh, to try and get rid of the line of fat round my middle. Then I'd quickly turn away! Blokes can't bear you to have that bulgy bit. So I figured it would be the same with my mates. They suggested I join them at this gym, for health reasons as much as for flab.'

Although gymnasium advertisements emphasise the health rather than the beauty, we felt it was only on the surface that a concern with feeling fit appeared to be a corrective to the male-controlled obsession with violent diets and flesh reduction. Underneath the new Fonda fitness ideology, lurk old stereotyped attitudes towards body and appearance.

As a test for real differences between the old and the new prescriptions for women's bodies, we looked at a typical bestseller from the seventies and compared it with the advice women are given by fashion and beauty magazines written in the eighties.

This is Marabel Morgan, author of the world bestseller, *The Total Woman* (1973): 'After your bath tonight, stand before the mirror and look at your body carefully. Say to that girl in the mirror, "I accept me as I am, bulges, hangups and all." It may not be as easy as it sounds, but it's so important. Face each *weakness* and realistically accept the fact that it exists. You're only human. You, as well as everybody else, have your *limitations*, so welcome aboard' (p.43 our emphasis).

Marabel Morgan does not even imagine that women could love their bodies. Women's bodies will have, she says, limitations, weaknesses, bulges and hangups. An extremely judgemental attitude towards female flesh: an attitude that carries with it inferences of necessary punishment and well-merited correction.

By contrast, Marabel Morgan's advice to women readers on how to react to their men's bodies is very different. In a chapter called 'Admire Him' she starts by reminding us that 'women need to be loved; men need to be admired. We women would do well to remember this one important difference between us and the other half' (p.57). She then offers her female audience a test. For a whole week, they are to do nothing but admire their men.

'Have you ever wondered why your husband doesn't just melt when you tell him how much you love him? But try saying "I admire you" and see what happens. If you want to free him to express his thoughts and emotions, begin by filling his empty cup with admiration. He must be filled first, for he has nothing to give until this need is met' (p.58).

When the Total Woman is totally exhausted with admiring her man's personality, she must then move onto his physique.

'Tell him you love his body. If you choke on that phrase, practise until it comes out naturally. If you haven't admired him lately, he's probably starving emotionally. He can't take too much at once, so start slowly. Give him one good compliment a day and watch him blossom right before your eyes' (p.61).

In the early seventies, Marabel Morgan, among many others, superlatively illustrated the contrast between the punishing horror-struck attitude women were expected to show towards their bodies and the fatuously fawning attitude they were expected to show towards male bodies. Women's bodies merited disgust. Men's bodies merited praise. A decade later, there have been outbreaks of feminism and fitness; but have our ideas really changed?

Women's magazines consistently offer self-punishment for flab and fat. In *Cosmopolitan* in October 1984, a regular feature called 'Your Body' contains the predictable question: 'Since the bad publicity given to dietary fat, I have reduced my fat intake as much as possible. I've lost a lot of unwanted flab and I would be feeling great except that my skin and hair have become very dry . . . What can I do about it?'

The answer does not, of course, tell the woman to keep hold of her unwanted flab, or even to want it. It suggests she introduces more fat into her diet. Significantly, next to this dietary advice is a half-page advertisement suggesting 'it takes more than a good diet to get you into shape'. Diets, it seems, can't stop women sagging and bulging. What is needed is thirty-five minutes every day with a punishing machine (called relaxing) which will tighten and firm up 'those SHAPE MAKING muscles'.

When we turned from beauty to health magazines, we found exactly the same principle, but neatly reversed. In *Here's Health*, June 1983, a six-page exercise schedule offered women benefits of nervous system co-ordination, greater alertness, decrease in stress, increase in coronary circulation, improved oxygen use, strengthened joint tissues, lowered metabolic rate, better quality sleep, ability to fight negative habits, and more positive feelings. All highly proper medical stuff, all in small print.

In bold black letters was the title: SHAPE UP FOR SUMMER. With it went the promise that all those exercises would not only increase your health but would decrease and improve you to a slimmer shape. The stress on the right mental attitude being the road to good health is still secondary to the end product of a finer figure.

The old idea that you tortured yourself to the stereotypical slimline never found official favour with feminists. However, the new prescriptions which wrap looks inside the health packages have found almost universal appeal – feminists included. Those who might have scoffed at the old notions of starving to lose a stone are now actually proud of spending £150 per annum (or more) to go to a gym three times a week, overtly for reasons of fitness but covertly to lose weight.

Listen to Nan, the lab technician we talked to earlier: 'I gave up fags. Put all my money into joining this gym. It costs more than

£200 a year. I go in lunch hours between experiments and after work. I am confident. In six months, I've lost a stone. And in the right places. I wouldn't have been caught dead going to Weight-Watchers, but I'm really excited about this gym.'

Although Nan gave up cigarettes, many women turn to smoking as a way of losing weight. Despite the publicity given to the relationship between smoking and cancer, many women we talked to would rather risk their lives than be fat.

This was Lynne's story: 'I gave up smoking once, for almost a year. I put on a lot of weight. Every time I wanted a cigarette I ate cheese instead, so it was understandable. My mother was very supportive. "You know you can lose weight," she kept saying. "Just find out you can give up smoking, then when that's out of the way, you can lose what you've put on. Pounds aren't permanent. But smoking can damage you." Of course, she was right. But my husband was very upset with me. He kept commenting on how ugly and unattractive I was. He kept saying, "I didn't marry a heavyweight ... a fatty. That wasn't in the contract." Then one night when we were going to a party, he suddenly said he couldn't go with me, I looked too awful. He was ashamed to be seen out with me. I was nine stone. I took up smoking that night. I was back to seven stone in a matter of weeks. I don't think I could give it up again, yet I know how bad it is for my health.'

We listened to women's conversations about illness and heard several remarks like, 'I was very seriously ill just after Tom was born. They thought I was going to die. One good thing about it though was I lost a lot of weight.'

We recognised the dangerous physical extremes women will go to. Anorexia nervosa, for instance, is one of our culture's most frightening diseases. The 1960s, the period in which this disease gained terrifying prominence amongst young women, was also the time when Weight-Watchers first opened their doors, soon followed by Overeaters Anonymous, Diet Workshops, Weight Losers' Institutes and organisations like Lean Line. By the mid 1970s there was an enormous growth in both Britain and the USA of saunas, gyms and lose-weight spaces. During exactly this same period, the women's liberation movement began asserting women's right to authority, autonomy, dignity and, above all, power.

This shows a clash of interest between one group of independent women who have acquiesced to men's mandate to reflect them physically to the extent that they can become hospitalised, and a second group of independent women, who, influenced by the feminist movement, feel less need to do so.

Kim Chernin (1981) is one writer who believes women's changing awareness has established these two movements: one toward female power, the other a retreat from it, supported by the fashion and diet industries. We feel the problem goes even further than Chernin pointed out. It is highly significant that for the last two decades, whilst one group of women went shyly to consciousness-raising groups to question women's subordinate role and try to change the shape of the world, another larger (in all senses) group rushed to Weight-Watching to deplore, agonise over and hope to change the shape of their bodies.

As our interviewees have shown, even feminists who resisted the more blatant calls to lose weight found it hard to resist the subtle edicts to reflect men by losing weight *inadvertently*. Many women have not admitted to us that in earlier years (usually before they became feminists) they were either dangerously anorexic or, which seems to us even more dangerous, victims of amphetamines.

Amphetamine addiction, publicised in the 1950s and 1960s as the speedy way to slim, is perhaps the most frightening, but least talked about, body phenomenon connected with the need to reflect men. Nan, the lab technician, who invested her cigarette savings in joining a gym, reluctantly talked about an earlier period when she had taken drugs to keep her weight down.

'I feel ashamed now. Then it seemed just another daring thing to try. My bloke really recoiled at fat figures. I wanted to please him. First, I took just five pills a day. Then more. Much more. At weekends, I was on really high doses. At first it was just to stop my appetite. Then I discovered they kept you awake and gave you this false sense of alertness. I reckoned I sounded brighter. He fancied me more. I upped the dose. I certainly got thin. But I also got very ill. I ate hardly anything and rarely slept. Finally, I freaked out. My senses became distorted, but I was too far gone to know what was happening. I was into fifteen or twenty a day when I began to get hallucinations. I was shit-scared. I'd been staying awake twenty hours or more so it wasn't surprising I was hooked and hallucinating. I saw people sitting in the trees outside the laboratory window. I tried to reach out to swing with them.

Once, I leapt out of the window. I was very badly injured. Of course, my bloke left me when I got into that kind of state. He didn't want to get caught with a hallucinating woman, dosed up on drugs, gradually going round the bend.'

Nan's situation was echoed by several of our interviewees. For many of them the experiences had been too painful, or were still too recent, for them to talk easily about it.

One of *us* knew exactly how Nan and the other women felt, from personal experience. Like many of the women who confided in her, Sally had been an amphetamine user for many years. Few of her friends or family were aware of exactly what was wrong with her, even during her worst periods. She still finds it hard to admit that she was an addict; even harder as a feminist to admit to the reasons. Here, after some struggle, is her story.

I started taking speed as part of a slimming series for the newspaper I worked on in the 1960s. It gave me a phoney 'lift' which at first seemed to have no ill effects. I continued to take pills intermittently to keep my figure down to the ideal implicitly specified by the professionals who monitored my fashion pages, and explicitly specified by several men in my personal life. I also began to depend on speed to give me a sense of false brightness, a round-the-clock alertness to match the big city social whirl that for years was my substitute for healthy living.

Whenever I grew nervous I took some of the pills, believing they would boost my confidence. I went openly to some doctors, secretly to others. I obtained several series of injurious prescriptions, some legal, some illegal. I stopped caring. I still desperately needed male approval, the more so as the stresses I lived under increased. I went from popping pills to having the stuff injected. I was by now seven stone, thin enough to show my body off in a bikini. But I had hideous marks and scars from the injections. I averted my eyes from the scars and my mind from the facts. My confidence did not increase.

Before I had embarked on this dangerous speed trial, I had been, by all accounts, a tidy, punctual, organised young woman. I had had fairly good eyesight, clear speech, was self-disciplined and would spend hours reading or writing. I had a bouncy but basically placid disposition. I was straightforward in my approach to other people.

Amphetamines changed all that. I began to lie to others and

then to myself about the pills I was taking. How many, how often, what they were and why. I began to mix the doses and step up the amounts. Anything for an extra high. I had regular prescriptions from several different doctors, none of whom knew about the others. When desperate, I knew two pushers who could get them for me. As long as I had the price, in cash.

I was, if only I had been brave enough to face the word, an addict.

Over the next twelve years, my faculties and behaviour went from being mildly eccentric to drastically distorted. I lost my sense of balance and some of my sight. My night vision was virtually non-existent. Before going to bed, I would have to light a candle and put it on the bedside table as I was unable to see in the dark. I slept so little that I was reduced to heavy doses of sleeping pills to counteract the effects of the amphetamines. At nights, I would also have to place a dry towel and some talc by the bed as I sweated continuously and would soak the sheets and my night-clothes in a few hours. This embarrassed me terribly and I took to having two or even three baths a day and washing my hair morning and evening. (I still wash my hair more often than anyone I know.) On even a short train journey, I would need a change of shirt and underwear as my clothes would be soaked through.

I became less able to concentrate and stopped reading almost entirely, but I continued to drive a car and to work, initially full-time, in the later years part-time. I had three very bad car crashes in two years, one with my child in the back of the car. After staying awake for twenty or thirty hours in the middle years, I would fall asleep at work. In the later periods I would faint or crash into deep comas, unable to be woken for several hours.

I developed what people took to be an idiosyncratic speech defect. This meant I spoke incredibly rapidly while at the same time slurring my words. It was no idiosyncracy. I had neither any control over it nor much awareness of what I sounded like. Most of the time I was in an agitated haze. I began to tell lies compulsively, to believe the best of my own fantasies.

As my personality slowly changed, my fears increased, but I clung obsessively to two false gods. 'I mustn't get fat,' I would say to myself. 'If I don't look right I won't be able to cope.' At other times, ill and exhausted, I would pull myself round by saying, 'I must keep awake. If I don't listen properly to what they are saying, they won't pay me any attention.' 'They' were still men.

In those years I wore expensive stylish clothes over an emaciated figure that I believed to be desirable. I stayed slim. I stayed awake. Somehow I directed or stage-managed shows or concerts, often without any sleep. I was still able to write, think and work with a mechanical measure of my former efficiency. A few years later, I lost my sense of navigation, my sense of time, and to a great extent my sense of reality.

To my own sad bewilderment I became as desperately unpunctual as I had once been rigidly punctual. And I didn't know why. As I could no longer read even the simplest road maps, I could no longer be relied on to turn up at the right places at the right times. I became an annoying and irritating joke to my limitlessly tolerant friends. In retrospect, I am amazed I had any friends left, or that I was fired from only one job in the space of fifteen years. That sacking was perhaps my most bitter experience.

After my second husband had left me and I was forced to bring up my child on my own, I decided to leave the South and the world of theatre and concerts and return to journalism which had once been my well-paid trade. With my excellent qualifications and a wealth of experience, I applied for, and was lucky enough to land, a prestigious job on a Northern newspaper. I grabbed hold of this chance and, taking my child, left our home and moved North, where we knew no one. I took on the job believing I was still a good writer who could meet any deadline.

It was no longer true. The drugs had beaten me. In my poor befuddled mind, I knew exactly what I wanted to say. I could see the stories set out on the page with my large steady black by-line underneath. It rarely happened. On paper, I could scarcely string three coherent sentences together. That was if I could make it to the typewriter at all. Among other things, I was arts editor, which meant writing reviews of artistic performances, late at night, to a very tight schedule.

I was terrified of going out alone in this strange Northern city. I couldn't find my way around. I could barely remember where my office was. I coaxed my best friend, M, to move North, to stay with me and my daughter, and to drive me to assignments. She stayed by my side while I muddled my way through interviews, or gathered a selection of ill-assorted facts, or saw three quarters of a show or concert. Then she drove me back to the office. There, faced with a typewriter and a terrifyingly close deadline, night after night, I failed to deliver the goods. Several times, while tears trickled down my face as much from disbelief as from despair, she offered to write my stories for me to try and save my job. In my arrogance and ignorance I refused to let her. I never raised the problem of pills with her or she with me.

The management were shocked, confused, and ultimately very angry. They felt they had paid a lot of money to obtain my services. I too was shocked, confused and ashamed. Only a few months after I had uprooted my child and myself from our home to make a new and successful start in the North, I was 'released' by the newspaper, put on the sick list of a stern, unfamiliar doctor, and left to deal with the problems of the expensive house I'd rented for a year, and the daunting intricacies of the DHSS supplementary benefit office.

The humiliation of this experience did not help me come off drugs ... if only because I was too far addicted to see the connection. Over the next few years, I daily and destructively drugged myself to be the half-person I still believed men approved of. I rarely allowed my body the rest it screamed for. Again and again I resorted to stimulants to keep awake, sedatives to crash to sleep. Outwardly strained, inwardly seething, refusing to recognise either state or concede natural remedies. The next day I would need more and different pills to keep going. The pattern painfully reinforced. The toll taken. Tranquillisers to mitigate gloweringly bad effects. Never calm. At the time it seemed to me odd that no amount of pills ever calmed me.

Behind my eyes a new hot redness surged. I would start to rage for no apparent reason. Some days I could not restrain myself from abusive outbursts. Once placid and good-humoured, now I was subject to fierce fits of violence. I turned wildly on even those who cared most for me. I hated myself as I did it – unable to stop.

I scared myself as much as I am sure I scared my friends. Two unbearably violent episodes tore apart the most stable relationship in my life at that time. I was so pepped up that I was barely aware of the crisis approaching and hardly noticed when it receded. So far was I from self-recognition that I began to rely more heavily than ever on pills to see me through each successive disaster.

Two incidents finally saved me. The first was being badly burnt in a farmhouse fire in the Lake District, an accident which was followed by a near fatal series of illnesses (including a liver disorder, kidney infection, severe head problems, and an ulcer) which finally overtook my worn-out body. Nine months of invalidism in the Lakes, nursed by M, my warm and attentive friend, were followed by eighteen months of spells in and out of hospitals, which though hard in themselves began to interrupt the consistency with which I was able to obtain and administer amphetamines.

It is ironic that my first relief from drugs came from an accident that burnt off my long hair, temporarily scarred my face and permanently erased an ear lobe. During this painful respite, I vowed (only a few times and only to myself) that I would try and come off them. But that first sigh of hope was weary. More a sigh of hopelessness. I had no real incentive. To be nursed back to health by my unselfish companion meant to return to the city; to the pills and to more self-destruction. The path away from drugs was still too tough for me to take. I was by now calling myself a feminist, but I still relied more on drugs and male approval than on women's strength or personal autonomy. I still discussed the problem with no one.

The second time I tried to give up amphetamines was in 1978. I met someone, a woman called B who cared enough about me to break through the silence and spend many patient months helping me to come off drugs.

Today that phrase 'coming off' sounds as easy as the phrase 'coming out'. Today, I realise sharply that only by enduring and surviving either experience (or in my case both), is it possible to comprehend with grim precision exactly how demanding are the realities behind the facile phrases.

In 1978 staying on drugs had become acutely dangerous; nevertheless it appeared preferable to and simpler than coming off. This meant that even with B (as with everyone in my past) initially I compromised, I lied, I clung hysterically to my hard-earned lethal supplies, which I secreted inside brown envelopes in my handbag. I carried that bag everywhere, even into the toilet, so that no one could ever firmly establish what if anything I was swallowing. B herself, innocently believing this to be merely another sign of my dramatic eccentricity, would not have thought of searching my possessions. I, however, had by then become frighteningly paranoid.

I did not only hang on to my handbag. I hung on also to fantasies about how my doctors decreed that high water retention necessitated constant injections. I hoped such tales would reason-ably account for my now frequent disappearances to the city and consequent scars on my arms, thighs and stomach when I returned. Ironically, although B did not believe these stories, not once did she suspect I was on drugs. In her love for me she began to fear for my life and had decided I had a rare and probably terminal illness which I was bravely refusing to reveal. A scrupu-lously moral person herself, she begged me to come clean, to act straightforwardly, above all to be honest.

Some remaining acuteness warned me that if I did not make this attempt to name the nameless, I could not sustain an honourable loving relationship nor retain any self-respect. Both were essential. I had reached the point where I had to try. I had to keep faith. With her. With myself.

B and I agreed that I should give up all attempts at paid work. She would temporarily support me (and our four daughters) while I rented an empty schoolhouse in order to try both to write – to write it out, and to live – to live it out . . . without the help of pills.

It was uphill the whole way back. I condemned myself to an unwilling dependency and an enforced isolation.

We lived in a small country village. Under pressure I gave up using my car, partly as a belated safety measure, partly to avoid the risk of escape to London where I could purchase more supplies. I had to minimise the risks. I had to allow myself to be driven to the small schoolhouse study in an adjoining village where there were no trains and few buses. The nearest city was eight miles away. It became a country prison where I committed myself for eight hours every weekday to recover and to relearn how to concentrate and how to write. In my mind the two became linked. Giving up drugs was an exercise which required the same iron will and self-discipline which was needed for writing.

Every morning the three elder girls went off cheerfully to their secondary school. My Charm was as cheery as the other two. Little Nic waited with B for me to get into their car. Not one of our four daughters had any idea that each breakfast-time brought with it a struggle between desire and principle. Between what I had to have and what I knew I could no longer afford.

Most days I would say, trying to sound casual: 'I think I'll take my old Triumph today. Give her a bit of a spin.' B never failed to read my mind. 'Don't do it, Sal. Don't drive. You are not fit yet.

Come in my car. Come with Nicky and me. We can drop you off. Try and write when we leave you. We'll pick you up again when school is over and work is finished. Hold on till then.'

B would put out an affectionate sustaining hand. Little Nic would smile waiting for me to decide. 'Come on, Sal. I like you coming with us. I can come and have tea with you at half past three. We can wait for Mum together then.'

Minimise the risks. Get in the car. Safe once inside. One more temptation temporarily past.

For the first three months of internment in the schoolhouse, time crawled. Minutes inched by. My hands shook on the typewriter keys. I sweated and had convulsions. Hardly surprising that I wrote little of interest. My thoughts were fixated on what I needed. I thought of little else. Except, sporadically, the fear of becoming fat. One fear exacerbated the other. I wanted them. Wanted them terribly. Could not say what I wanted. Could not write what I wanted. Could not write.

One morning I told B I could not last out. I should have to quit the experiment. I had already secretly sent off for more pills and asked for them to be posted to the schoolhouse address. I did not have her guts.

'You have your own strength. I believe in you. Take my cigars, they may help. I want to try and help you. Try one more day. Try writing about it. Writing about it may help.'

Would it? Would anything? I doubted if anything could help. It had been a long time. Thirteen years on and off. Rarely off. (Later I told a doctor that it had been 'at least four years' – that was the most I could face admitting to.) I needed help. Needed someone close. But I had never asked for help before, never acknowledged the need for the needle. If not the steel-sharp sensation the needle produced then at least its substitute: the green and pink pills. Even today if I enter a stranger's bathroom, I have to stop myself rooting through their bathroom cabinet in case, just in case, they too might have a concealed tin of the bluey-greens, or the double-strength pinks.

On the day that became a turning point, Charm was doing her French homework at the breakfast table. The pains in my head were bad. My legs and hands were trembling. My need of the pills. My daughter's need of me. 'Mummy what is *"aide moi"*?' Charm asked. 'It means "help me", Charm,' I replied steadily.

But I was not steady. Not then. Not later. Alone in the

schoolhouse I typed the words 'Help me'. A hard phrase for me to write, and I shrank from writing it. Better to write than to give in. Better to smoke than to give in. I opened the packet of small black cigars. Write what I need. Write it before the first of B's small black cigars burns out. I remember watching the end of the last cigar burn slowly in the stainless steel ashtray I had brought from home. I could not use the fragile china ashtrays in the sedate schoolhouse for that kind of smoking. The kind that was to go on all day. Word after word. Sentence after sentence. Cigar after cigar. I remember writing: 'This smoking is to help me from going back. To help keep me from going back on.' Long pause. 'Back on . . . drugs. SAID IT. I've said it. Write it again.'

It was the first breakthrough. It had been better to smoke than to give in. To give up. But already I knew I should in the end also have to give up smoking. Smoking stops the appetite. Dangerous thought. Better to eat than to half-live like I had. Better even to be . . . Resist, even now, writing the word 'fat'. Better to try. I had never tried before. I had always given in but had not known that I was giving in. I had always kidded myself that I would take only a few greens. A couple of pinks. I would be moderate. Reasonable. But wanting them is not reasonable. It is not safe. It never stops there. Always goes on. Always more. Wanting more. Back on the road. Away from being able to feel properly. See clearly. Think lucidly. Away from writing. From loving. From honesty.

I knew all this but still I encountered setbacks. One morning I slipped away from the typewriter and found the scales. Weighing myself, I began to worry again. A few months off (and on) pills and I was putting on weight. I wanted the stuff so badly I contemplated hiring a car and driving to London but forced myself back to the typewriter. Then I began to think about eating. Eating. More eating. Hate. Hate myself fat. Hate myself ugly. Fat *is* ugly. Usually thin. Drugged up. High. Bad-tempered. Raging. Mad. Glad. *Stop it*. Stupid.

By then I knew it *was* stupid to want that crazed feeling of excitement. That thin spiral of high pleasure, nerve-end tension, rushing through my bones, till dry-mouthed it cracked jagged somewhere inside my head. Red. Raging red and powerful.

I had to try and forget. I had to try and concentrate on the words. Before each cigar burnt out I had to try and locate the correct words then pin them to the page. Some days I wished I could talk about it to other women. I was not able to. It was too early. But it was something for me to have scribbled inadequately about it. Something to have written it at all. A slight admission.

It may take many more slight admissions from many more women whose bodily desires to reflect men have led them to become drug addicts before we can begin to put this right. But a few women have made a start. A few women feel hopeful. A few women we talked to recognised that in order to stay off speed *they have to accept that sometimes they are fat and that it does not matter.*

It continued to matter to me throughout the months when my enforced incarceration gradually became a willing and fruitful solitude.

It mattered less as I slowly regained my physical and mental health. Today I am once more tidy, punctual and well organised. Like all converts, I am said by my friends to be rigidly and annoyingly so. Today I once more have the use of my writing skills and most of my faculties. I have been exceedingly fortunate. But the way back has had bleak moments. The most painful has been to face what I was. And what I constantly fear I could again be. An addict. If you have had to face that you no longer worry if you are size fourteen rather than size ten.

5

THE MANDATORY SMILE AND THE OBLIGATORY ORGASM

Smiles and orgasms are two of the most significant gestures women make. And still, these aspects of women's behaviour, like the others so far investigated, operate on the same rule: they are organised to please men.

On the street men appreciate, indeed, they *demand*, women's smiles. In bed they appreciate their orgasms. Both in public and private women exist to please men. This means their emotions, like their bodies, are not truly their own. Women cannot afford valid or honest expressions of feeling.

We overheard two teenage girls discussing clitoral versus vaginal orgasms. The girls decided that as boys prefer to think girls have vaginal orgasms, girls may as well let them continue to think so. These teenagers seemed to us to be extremely knowledgeable about sexual experience, as well as about boys' preferences. The way they proved that the Freudian-dictated vaginal orgasm was neurologically non-existent would have gladdened Masters' and Johnson's hearts. (see Masters and Johnson, 1966). But the way they decided to pretend that they had had them, despite the evidence of their own bodies, somewhat saddened our hearts. Obviously fashions in sexuality change, but styles of behaviour that reap good, solid male acclaim do not change so easily.

When we talked to women about these emotions, we discovered a contradiction. Signs like smiling and orgasms should express the freely given responses of free women; emotions like laughter, contentment, joy, humour, even ecstasy. But for most women, most of the time, they don't.

Geneviève Dariaux (1967) who writes about smiles in her book *The Men In Your Life*, says that 'all women know they *ought* to smile but how many smile with their eyes as well?' (p.282). Many of the women we talked to bore out her words. Several of our interviewees had experiences similar to those of Paula, a school-teacher:

'As a child, I was always being told to run and greet my father with a big smile. Mum would say: "Dad's had a hard day, Paula. He needs us to make him feel better." I used to wonder why Dad never smiled back at Mum. After all she'd had a pretty hard day too with five of us kids to look after.'

But, as Geneviève Dariaux points out, 'important men do not smile very often unless they are in politics' (p.282). Our interviewees felt that all the men they knew saw themselves as important, so we could go further than Geneviève Dariaux and suggest that all men (even the unimportant) do not smile often. Unless *they* want to. For men, smiling is a spontaneous act, a mark of enjoyment, appreciation or self-satisfaction. Men do not smile because they feel they should. They certainly don't smile in order to please the other sex.

For women, smiling is mandatory. Women smile when they feel like scowling. Some even smile when they feel sad, if it helps cheer men up, increases their sense of self or if it wards off their anger. Some women put on their smile when they put on their make-up. Other women who don't wear make-up wear a smile instead. But it is as highly coloured and artificial as the cosmetics they have rejected. Women are trained to smile in the workplace, even if they are taking time to talk to women friends and a man decides to interrupt them. Paula talked about the school where she works:

'When a man barges in on two women talking in the staff room, not only does he expect us both to be polite and allow him to change the subject to something he cares about, but he also expects us both to smile welcomingly at him. I hate to admit this, but every time I am in that situation that's exactly what I do!'

Women who live with men learn to smile at them in the home. It seems that women smile even more if for a moment they have been 'guilty' of turning their attention away from their boyfriend or husband. Valerie, for example:

'I used to spend most of my time with the children or seeing my mum, and generally smiling at Brian to keep the peace. But recently, I've gone to a few women's meetings. Brian feels dreadfully excluded. He hates me going, and gets very irritable. So I try and choose a time when he is out too, so he won't have to babysit. I rush back to get in before him and put on a big smile and pretend he is the most important feature in my life. That smile deflects his anger for a bit.'

That many women like Valerie use smiles to wriggle out of trying situations was wittily pointed out by Ingrid Bengis (1974) when she said, 'One of these days, I'm going to put band-aid across my mouth so that smiling will become less of a reflex in uncomfortable situations' (p.30).

What we discovered was that even more women use smiles to try and *avoid* difficult or even dangerous confrontations. Women know from hard practical experience that smiling takes time, is arduous work, and is an essential part of the elaborate ritual of reflection in which women are forced to dissemble. If they fail to do so, they reap heavy penalties. As Dale's smile experiment showed, when women don't smile men become wildly, even violently, abusive.

Ruth, who is a waitress in a large Penzance café, complained: 'Smiling is the worst part of my duties. Men put you down or even complain to the boss if you don't grin at them when you bring their sausages and beans. Two of my mates were fired this season for not smiling enough. One customer was so bloody rude to one girl, she could have mashed his face into his plate of spuds! She didn't. Instead she held herself back, served him without a word, but simply couldn't bring herself to smile sweetly at him. He complained. She lost her job. Her friend, who was sent to serve him, was so upset that she could not smile either. She got the push too.'

For twentieth-century white women, the smile is the equivalent of the nineteenth-century black servants' shuffle. It is an indication that a victim is acquiescing in her own oppression. Women are encouraged to show their cheerful compliance on their faces.

We know from history that oppressed groups have always been made to smile. Those in power need the flattery and supportive laughter of subordinates as a constant reassurance that their power is rightfully held. Today it occurs in factories, offices and boardrooms. Some of us have watched subordinates forcing an agreeable (and agreeing) grin up at their superiors . . . and not letting rip until they reach the canteen! If we are less lucky, we have been those subordinates, playing that game. For many women, these glued-on grins have become necessary tools. Like the tinkle of their laughs, they are part of a plastic armour. So often, smiles symbolise not enjoyment but consent to being discriminated against.

As we see it, the problem is that each woman's fake smile helps to maintain the oppressed state of her sisters. This behaviour has got to stop somewhere and soon. A few brave women should refuse to smile unless *they* want to. And brave they will have to be, for, as Virginia Woolf pointed out, when women do not look delighted to see men, the men's capacity for life diminishes; as that capacity wanes, the strong-arm tactics are likely to increase.

Abbey's story illustrates what can happen. She used to be married to a famous London photographer who preferred to overlook her keen brain and excellent economics degree and use her as a face and legs model for his fashion photos. 'I married Terry when I was twenty-two years old. At the beginning, I looked up to him and was always smiling and pleased to see him. Then he demanded I gave up my business management job and worked for him on a series called The Laughing Lovelies. He told me: "It's your figure what counts not your damn figures. So keep your clever-clever views to yourself and smile. Remember, you are married to someone in the public eye." '

Everything went well as long as Abbey did not criticise him. 'But if I put on what he called my serious smart-ass look he would get very angry and sometimes he threatened to swipe me,' she told us. The first time she had a serious argument with Terry, about the amount of light needed in a photo, he carried out his threat. 'But it was only in the neck where it didn't show much. The problem was that I was still crying when we walked into the magazine office and that made Terry angrier. He told me to cheer up and smile because we were on display.' Once, before a social gathering, Abbey remained adamant about a financial matter. He blacked her eye in fury, and then said: 'You know I am sorry, don't let me down. It is a public occasion and I need you to smile.'

Abbey's story – sadly, it is not an extreme case – is an apt illustration of the fact that male power is maintained and manifested by a pervasive cluster of forces that range from control of women's consciousness to physical abuse. The process of reflecting men is one means of that control of consciousness. And women's accept-ance of that control shows in their acquiescent grins.

If the mandatory smile is part of the day-time uniform of the women who enhance men's images by sublimating their own feelings, it is the *obligatory orgasm* which has become an equally important part of their night-time apparel. Nor does it seem to matter if that orgasm is real or fake.

'It's easier to fake it than face the awful inquisition afterwards,' said Sonia, speaking for a large group of married women we interviewed in the West Country. 'If we don't pretend we've had one they say we're frigid. Or holding back on purpose just to get back at them!'

'As if we would!' said Brigid, another one of the group, with a giggle. Jessie laughed too, but then said seriously: 'You've got to fake to make them feel secure. Sort of superior. Sex is definitely their weak spot. You have got to make them feel good in bed. If you don't, they might take it out on you.'

The orgasm, as much as the statutory smile, is a significant symbol of John Stuart Mill's 'willing slave' in today's society. Slaves shuffle, and women perform pleasantly, because they have no choice. Many of the women we spoke to grin and bear it during the day; others fake and feign it at night.

Lesley, mother of two small children, recently separated and on the dole, said: 'When they are paying the rent it's very hard to tell them to piss off. I found it even harder not to give them what they want sexually . . . even if I had to pretend. Maybe it's just me . . .'

Betty, who was older than the others, said wearily: 'It's not just you, kiddo. I've faked all my married life. I've never had a job or money of my own so it's always been best to humour him like. Some nights I wish orgasms didn't exist then I might have enjoyed sex better. Years ago, it wasn't so bad. I was more up to it, he wasn't so nattery. With him getting older and with all those sex books about, it's made it worse. Trouble is nowadays it's not enough for *them* to have one, they practically insist on you having one too, even if you're working out the Co-op list in your head while he's humping up and down! Just because the sex liberation books tell them that all women can have multiple orgasms, the blokes want us all to shout and rave and heave about to make their egos feel good.'

We feel it is ironic that the media image of the 'liberated woman' is being used by men to pressure women into a male-defined sexuality. However, the women themselves are not so easily taken in.

Take Janice, eighteen years of age and just married: 'Someone ought to tell them that if a women really does have an orgasm she goes all stiff and quiet. You don't have to rave or shift about at all. But if any of us lot told 'em that, it would blow their minds. As far as I'm concerned, having orgasms the way *they* like it is important to keep them sunny side up.' Janice said she learnt that piece of wisdom from the three men she went out with before she got married.

'What they taught me was you mustn't let them get ratty because you never know what they'll do to you. They'll sure as anything knock you about. One bloke cut me up quite badly, there was blood everywhere on me mum's nice white sheets. Just because I wouldn't have one. Still, he was a bit over the top about sex.

'The next one gave me a belting when I didn't come, and I told him it was his fault. He said I'd made him feel less of a man . . . Well after that I thought, "Give this up for a lark, Janice, time to settle down with one steady bloke and do it his way." So I got married. Now I fake as a matter of course and he never cuts up rough.'

Listening to Janice and her friends, some wry lines of Robin Morgan's come back to us: 'Each sister faking orgasms under the System's very concrete bulk at night to survive' (1972, p.64). For survival lies at the root of many of these sexual pretences.

It is a sad reflection of our society that orgasms, like smiles, should be yet another way women feel forced to pleasure and flatter men. Orgasm in a free society should express ultimate sexual excitement, the exquisite feeling of senses pinpointed to meet flesh, the physical truth of love or passion. But in our social world, male-dominated and ideologically heterosexual, female orgasms are too often physical gestures that lie. They are gestures of a manipulated heart pressed into male supportive service. This is the price today's women are paying for the increasingly high priority set on sex in a patriarchal society. Sally Kempton (1978) was correct when she said 'Constance Chatterley was a male invention. Lawrence invented her, I used to think, specifically to make me feel guilty because I didn't have the right kind of orgasms' (p.445).

Julie, an Australian housewife, who was softly spoken and admittedly soft-hearted, said: 'I always have a great desire to make things go smoothly. I want to make my relationships with men gentle, so I am often tempted to fake an orgasm just to be nice and warm towards a man I love. Even if the man isn't pressuring me, I tend to feel guilty if I don't have an orgasm.'

" SOMETHING'S WRONG, ISN'T THERE, DIANA?
YOU NEVER FAKE MULTIPLE ORGASMS ANYMORE. "

Mona, who spoke to us about her children, was much harder: 'Most men need treating like children in bed. They thrust their need for orgasm on you just like a child demanding nurturing. You're supposed to fake it, if necessary, to comfort them for their often useless masculinity! Well, I won't do that any more. I've gone on sex strike. So they try to make me feel guilty as hell. I'm a woman, not every man's mother for goodness sake!'

Sexual liberation, the optimistic slogan of the 1960s, seems to have become just another bondage in the 1980s. Female orgasms, real or fake, have become a given part of our social reality. They are the mainstay of the necessary nurturing mechanism by which all heterosexual women support all men.

Jilly Cooper (1969) believes that 'women are like machines, the more they are used the better they work' (p.70). In her view, making love becomes the cornerstone of marriage (p.62). She says that if you 'keep your partner happy in bed, he will be unlikely to stray' (p.62). She really believes that 'because men basically like to boss, and women to be bossed . . . you may find it difficult to say no when he says "Come to bed with me" ' (p.51). Although Jilly Cooper accepts that 'it's not vital to have an orgasm every time you go to bed with a man' she adds sagely that 'the fact remains that it's much nicer if you do' (p.62).

Unlike us, she fails to ask the question: nicer for whom? And she emphasises that 'a woman should be grateful that her husband wants her, and any woman who says "I don't feel like it tonight" more than two days running, unless she's ill, pregnant or recovering from a baby, deserves to have an unfaithful husband' (p.66). Jilly Cooper is not alone in her beliefs, as is evident from *The Hite Report* (1976), that monumental study of female sexuality. Significantly, *The Hite Report* does not ask women if they fake orgasms. It *assumes* that they do. Shere Hite says the idea that it doesn't matter, 'if women have orgasms or not is an absurd lie women tell themselves.'

We would point out that it is in men's interests that women believe this lie. We were interested to see whether her study confirmed any of our recent findings in this area of sexuality and it most certainly does. She says that all women 'are made to feel they must have orgasms more to please the man than to please themselves' (p.130); the women she interviewed certainly backed up this view. One woman told her she did it to make her man feel successful. Another said she 'performed' to 'boost his ego' as well as his love for her (p.130). Women, it seemed, didn't like being performers but did it because they felt judged by the men and also judged themselves harshly if they didn't have orgasms (p.130).

Like so many of the women we talked to, most of those in the Hite study said if they didn't 'come', it proved he wasn't a real man. So they either upped the decibel range of their genuine response, or they made do with a fabricated one. Davina, one of *our* most articulate interviewees, told us: 'He enjoys watching me, so I try and give him a good show. I've even learnt how to make my vagina contract at will, to give him a good time. I enjoy the whole thing immensely and so does he. It is no trouble for me to be nice to him like that.' We wished all the women we had talked to had found it as effortless to be nice and had got as much out of their relationships. This did not, however, seem to be common.

Petra is one woman who spent years being nice to her husband while he spent that same time consistently putting her down. Finally, she stopped playing by his rules: 'We had three children and I didn't want any more. I wanted to do something for myself, so I started an Open University course. What with that and the kids, I began to spend less time telling John how clever and witty he was. As soon as I started studying, he began making sardonic cracks about me in front of the children and our friends. They'd laugh with embarrassment and he'd say, "Why don't you smile Petra?" I tried to smile and to be nice to him, both because I truly loved him and because I was afraid of getting pregnant again before my first exams. But with all that studying and housework, I was often too tired to flatter him in bed where he needed it most. So he started hitting me. Said I wasn't paying him enough attention. He got me pregnant again. I became really frightened and realised it's backing up your man all the time no matter what your man does. You have to back him up everywhere even in the privacy of your own bed. You must lie with your own body if they need it. John needed me to be his resource, his sexual resource. I think they all need that. I was faking as often as I could manage it. I learnt if I didn't come up with the right response in bed he might hit me. I realised even the most civilised men sometimes do it. Even when they say they love you. It's very confusing. John was a very civilised person, very witty and cultured, not the sort of man you'd think would do it. It was hard to go on being nice.'

Petra's story, of a woman worn out after ten years spent smiling and being 'nice' to a man who neither appreciated it nor reciprocated it, except with cruelty, is a frightening illustration of an idea recently put forward by Arlie Russell Hochschild (1983): she calls smiling 'emotional labour' (p.7). This is as relentless as physical labour, as demanding as intellectual labour, but it passes largely invisibly and goes mainly unrewarded and is carried out, of course, predominantly by women. In her book *The Managed Heart: Commercialisation of Human Feeling*, Hochschild interviewed flight attendants on a big American airline who were paid to smile. She spent months observing these trainee air-hostesses whose day started with the pilot telling them: 'Now girls, I want you to go out there and really smile. Your smile is your biggest asset. I want you to go out there and use it. Smile. Really smile. Really lay it on' (p.4). By the end of a day delivering paid chuckles, simpers and smirks to difficult and demanding passengers, mainly men, the weary cheery who had spent hours keeping the airline's promise of real happiness and calm were as frayed, tense and tired as the housewives and mothers we talked to. Like our interviewees, these air-hostesses had to 'manage' their emotions in such a way that the very act of manipulating feelings became a frightening integral part of the emotion.

Arlie Hochschild calls the process which ensues a war of smiles. In this way the fatigued and battle-scarred victims are ironically the smile-sellers themselves – women like Petra and Abbey and Valerie and Paula. Arlie Hochschild feels that emotional labour is similar to housework, taking up an equal amount of time, receiving as little recognition, something over which women have little choice. She says although we depend on it like housework, we take it for granted, and the fact that there hasn't been a word for it up till now is significant (p.167).

We feel that the process of reflecting men is one that involves *all* women in the daily acts of deference that become transformed into 'emotional work' in the private arena and 'emotional labour' in the public arena. And we would go even further than Arlie Hochschild and suggest that obligatory orgasms should be added to mandatory smiles as the tools of the compulsory cheerfulness with which women are expected to carry out this emotional servicing.

From our interviews it seems that this kind of unpaid labour, which she calls 'the womanly art of status enhancement' (p.171), helps to keep the patriarchal system running smoothly. It takes time – women's time – and drains women's already scant resources. These smiles and fake orgasms are the essential characteristics of an emotional labour structure which is attached to a system of reflecting men.

Of course, as Arlie Hochschild knows, not only air-hostesses are professional purveyors of emotional labour. Roughly half the women who work have jobs that call for this kind of emotional labour. These jobs are mainly in the service sector where there is enormous emphasis on deference. These occupations include secretaries who maintain cheerful offices; waitresses who create congenial eating atmospheres; the caring, nurturing, supportive posts of nurses, health workers, librarians and teachers; and the artificially warm, witty and welcoming ranks of TV and radio announcers. We spoke to women in many of these jobs and found that all these occupations need a conspicuous and conscious caring attitude – a manipulated concern which becomes the commercial distortion of a managed heart. It is not surprising then to discover that most of these jobs are done by women, who merely continue in public the emotional work they perform in private. The world turns to women for mothering, nurturing, and this fact silently attaches itself to a great many job descriptions, at considerable cost to the women concerned.

Hochschild's flight attendants were taught how to suppress their anger if passengers insulted them and, instead, display a friendly disposition (p.33). This meant that they were forced to express feelings which were out of tune with what was genuinely demanded by the situation. Similarly, Ruth, our Penzance wait-ress, was supposed to smile when the situation demanded she mash a customer's face into his plate of food and Petra, who was exhausted and needed sleep, was saddled with a husband who expected her to manage a few simple orgasms.

Of course, to some extent, both women and men do emotional work, both at home and in their jobs. But it is patently not as important to men as it is to women, nor is it important in the same ways, nor is it done for the same reasons. Above all, it is only women who make a job out of emotional work in the cause of faithfully and flatteringly endorsing male authority. The over-riding reason that women manipulate their emotions more than men is the fact that in general they have less independent access to money, power, authority or status in society. Their position as a subordinate social group crucially determines the amount of time and energy they give to managing their emotions in order to build up men's egos. Because they lack other resources, women make a resource out of feeling. And men know this and can take advantage of it. Remember Petra asserting that John needed her to be his resource even when he was hitting her about. We talked to many women in similar situations expressing the same senti-ments. This means that a woman's capacity to manage her feelings and engage in this kind of manipulatory emotional work is considerably more important than it would be for a man.

When Arlie Hochschild discusses the particular social condi-tions which make emotion management more prevalent amongst the female sex, she suggests that specialisation of emotional labour rests on the different childhood training of the heart that is given to girls and boys (p.163). We can certainly confirm her tentative suggestion with our very positive findings (in Chapter Two) which show how well and how early girls are taught the message of reflecting men.

One conclusion Arlie Hochschild comes to which bears strikingly upon our theme is how women react to subordination by making defensive use of their sexual beauty, charm and relational skills in a way that allows these qualities to become vulnerable to commercial exploitation. As we have already shown, in Chapter Three, it is also the use of these qualities for survival purposes which exposes women to private as well as to public exploitation.

Are women themselves aware that the emotional labour they perform means they have to suppress or negate real and possibly conflicting feelings of their own? Certainly women like Brenda seem very well aware of it. Brenda lives on a large housing estate outside Peterborough, with a small child and a husband who leaves at seven o'clock every morning to travel to work. Twice a week she does a half-day's work as a clerk while another woman on the estate minds her child.

'Some days I think my face will set like jelly into the fixed smile I put on as Jim leaves. It's still there for the milkman who's a surly bugger and never smiles back and for the postman who seems to expect a welcome before he hands over the letters. I even smile at the catalogue man, who gives me the creeps. At work, the bloke in charge expects all five of us women to be jolly all the time despite the fact the work is boring, badly paid and most of us can't stand him. But we all do it.' Brenda says that at night she's sometimes so tired she feels like crying when Jim comes home but she never shows it. 'All the women on our estate know you have to perk up and smile when they get in. You know you have to perk up in bed too whatever you're feeling like.'

We asked Brenda whether smiling and simulating a sexual response when she didn't feel like it made her feel closer to Jim. 'Oh no! No, not at all! The more I do it the more I feel kind of cut off from him, and from myself. I even feel cut off from the other women round here who I know are doing it too. It's not like something we're proud of sharing. The more I smile and try and perk up in bed, the worse the cut-off feelings get. It's funny really because I thought acts like that were about caring for people. Well, they are in a way. But they don't connect me to the people I'm supposed to love. I'm not sure what's happening to me because I don't feel close to Jim anymore, or to anyone.'

Petra, who had spent over ten years faking emotions for John's benefit, was even clearer about the consequences of her emotional manipulation. 'Every time I faked I felt distanced from him and from myself. Although I also think phoney orgasms can be a woman's way out, if you need one. If orgasms are just part of sex that's demanded of you, and you're forced to fake either to make them feel better, or because you're afraid of what they'll do to you, then faking becomes a way of keeping your real self apart. The trouble is you finally end up distanced even from yourself. Oh dear, I don't want to talk about it, it's humiliating and I feel lonely.'

The acknowledgements of women like these not only strengthen Arlie Russell Hochschild's idea that emotional labour carries with it increasing self-estrangement and isolation, but goes beyond her findings. Whereas she had primarily concentrated on the surface emotion of artificial smiles, we asked our interviewees also to take into account the possibly deeper rooted effects of producing false sexual behaviour.

Let Venetia sum it up for us in her compelling and unique way: 'You don't know the way you're behaving is false, not when you're doing it, or not before you go to evening classes and mix with women who talk about things like that. When you're like I was, a girl with no opinions of your own, which was what Marcus drove me to, you just know sex is behaving in a slave way to him, anytime he asks for it, *him being kind of king*. That's what Marcus thought he was. Of course, he was a class above me, you can tell by his name. His mum named him after some Roman emperor and ever since he was a child he thought of himself as hero-like and was a great one for pushing and shoving me about, me being lower than him, especially in bed. And especially if you didn't do it right, or worse if you didn't do it at all. You had to be sure you said all the right things about him and sex or else he'd turn nasty with his hands and it would be the worse for you.'

Venetia explained that she had to pretend, 'or it will never be over, what they call passionate love and you know is all that rigmarole, dirty, and sometimes belting you before they go back to playing pool.'

What effect did the constant pretence have on a girl like Venetia? 'Faking all the time leaves you without any feelings of your own. It made me really sorry because I loved him at the start. But I never had any feelings of my own, not the whole time I lived with Marcus, not even when I got engaged to him which puts a girl up a rung. I never had any opinions of my own either in those days so it was hard to tell if I was on the right track with all that faking. I couldn't tell my mates, well you don't, do you, when your mum brings you up not to talk about those sort of things?'

Venetia's isolation was the strongest element in her suffering. But she was sad also because what had been genuine emotion was reduced to a sham. And she knew it.

Like many women we spoke to Venetia started smiling and faking for good, kind motives. To create a happier home. A pleasanter atmosphere. To make things go well. But she grew bitter as she watched behaviour that started with the best possible intentions fade into acts that were immoral. Actions that were not true to the emotions felt. Actions performed with the hope of something better. Or from fear of something worse.

We feel many men are like Marcus, flight passengers demanding constant contentment; and many women, like Venetia, are air-hostesses selling smiles, suffering stress. Stress at not being true to themselves. Stress at trading in false sexual expression. Abbey and Venetia and the others are not alone. Nor are they different from the rest of us. We have probably all done it in our time; exchanged truth for security. Maybe to keep our children. Maybe to increase our incomes. At rock bottom, most women know that the price of being 'feminine' and approved of in a male supremacist society is to be a liar.

That's why each day women sell their souls with smiles. Each night they barter their spirits with orgasms. Each time it happens there is the promise of buying them back with the coin of male approval. But there is never a guarantee.

6

GIVING IT AWAY

Why do women reflect men?

The common explanation seems to be that women reflect men because women are financially dependent upon men; that women are nice to men as a means of getting money from men; that because so many women rely on men for financial support they are concerned to maintain the physical and emotional health of the breadwinner – so that the support continues.

There is also a general acknowledgement that a woman must 'keep the man' who provides the money. While *his* job may be to keep her, in terms of board and lodging, *her* job is often viewed as one of keeping him – from straying. And this too can lead to a lot of ego-massaging behaviour. For it is not unlikely that a man should prefer to come home to, and stay with, a woman who caters to his needs and makes him feel good.

These explanations function as the ground rules for many women's magazines where women are urged to look after men in relation to everything from cholesterol-free food to a reduction in stress, with more than fleeting advice about the values of sexual stimulus on the way. But it is not just between the pages of women's magazines that these understandings can be found; they are the ones put forward by women themselves.

Many of the women we interviewed made the links between their treatment of men and their own economic dependence without hesitation. There were women who openly and cheerfully acknowledged that you had to 'butter up a man' if you wanted money – for anything from a new dress to shoes for the kids, and women who were more circumspect, but who still made it quite clear that the principle in operation is *he who feels good pays more.* Understandably, a lot of effort went into making men feel good so that they would pay more; understandably, too, a lot of women were not always comfortable with the recognition of what they were doing and why.

'It's one of the reasons women are seen as manipulating,' one woman said, 'because you can't come out and demand money. You can't even ask for it sometimes. You have to be clever about getting it.' And many women agreed.

Yet this topic is rarely discussed among women and certainly not in the presence of men. Such silence could suggest that for many it could be better if much were left unsaid. This is a plausible explanation given that we met with many unsolicited admissions that it was a shame that women were required to resort to such shabby behaviour in order to survive. But for all the women who were unhappy about the way they felt they were obliged to relate to men, there were also women who had no qualms of conscience; and there were women who were posi- tively proud of their own performance. That these women did not publicly talk about what they did – and why – seemed to have more to do with their reluctance to divulge some of the 'trade secrets of femininity' than with any discomfort about their own behaviour.

One topic women did talk about voluntarily, and at length, was the relative poverty of women, and it came as something of a surprise to discover just how well informed so many women are about unequal educational opportunities, unequal work and unequal pay opportunities. This was not the only source of poverty that women quoted and criticised. Virtually every woman commented on the poverty of 'single parent families' (almost invariably headed by women), the increasing number of women who from choice or necessity were rearing children on their own, without the financial assistance of a man and with great financial difficulty.

The recognition among women that they are poor is one which has considerable statistical support. During the 1975–1985 Decade on Women, the United Nations was concerned to raise the world's consciousness about the plight of women, and published the following facts and figures based on the information provided by the member states:

Women
constitute *half* the world's population
perform nearly *two thirds* of the world's work
receive *one tenth* of the world's income
own less than *one hundredth* of the world's wealth.

So men are rich and women are poor. And according to the United Nations and other responsible economic agencies and individuals, each year men are getting richer and women are getting poorer, so that it has been predicted that by the year 2000, poverty will be almost exclusively a female problem; hence the term 'the feminisation of poverty' (see Hilda Scott, 1984).

In the face of such statistical evidence there can be no debate about the existence of women's poverty: clearly, the world over, women are pitifully poor. For less than 10% of the world's wages and less than 1% of the world's wealth is simply not enough to go round. Excellent money managers though women may be, they cannot keep themselves and their children on such a small allowance. This is why women must have access to the 99% of wealth controlled by men. This is why women are in the business of managing the emotions of men. This is why women are led to say what men want to hear – rather than what women think.

It would be a mistake to assume that women are only, or even primarily, pleasing the men they live with in order to procure a rise in pay, however. Women are dependent on the bounty of men in all sorts of situations: from the daughter who persuades the father to be forthcoming with some form of finance, to the secretary, sales assistant or waitress who must serve and salve the sensitivities of the customer *and* the boss, there is the widespread recognition that men control the money and that one way for women to obtain a bigger share (which they often desperately need) is to be sweet to the paymaster.

The majority of women are aware that it is not just a matter of being nice to men; they understand that there is some sort of trade going on between the sexes. This is particularly so when a woman is being directly supported by a man: she is not necessarily just being her pleasant and polite self when she shows her concern and consideration for his finer feelings. Instead, it can be that she is fulfilling her side of the bargain. In return for his manly and responsible breadwinning contribution she is expected to do the womanly things: to be the homemaker, to provide the services

– good cheer, a good ear, and often a good time. If she did not carry out these tasks – if she did not increase the stature and wellbeing of the man – she could be judged a failure. Either 'selfishness' or 'stupidity' could be advanced as the reason she did not deliver her part of the bargain.

While the 'trading laws' might be relatively rigid and allow little room for manoeuvre, not *all* the women we interviewed resented this aspect of the relationship between the sexes. There were some who expressed their satisfaction with what they say as the set 'rates of exchange'. They were prepared to put their energies into a man partly because they believed that they were getting a fair deal. And the bargains they struck were not always or only financial: 'Sure, I'm financially dependent and it makes a big difference. But I'd like to think I'd still be nice to my husband – that I'd prop him up a bit and make him feel important – even if I could pay my own way. Because I like him. And I like what we have together. And it wouldn't last very long if I didn't put some effort into making our relationship work.'

It would prove to be difficult to separate the elements of the economic relationship from the emotional relationship, for the two are so often elaborately intertwined. One 'economically inactive' and dependent woman acknowledged that she managed the emotions of her husband and that there had to be sufficient love and management to prevent him from 'looking elsewhere'. So not only did she want home to be the place where he would get the nurturance he would find nowhere else in the hostile world, not only did she want to ensure that she gave the quality of nurturance that no one else could provide but she also worked to make her husband *dependent* on that emotional support. 'I can't live without him,' she said with explicit reference to his financial support, 'so I have to make sure he can't live without me.' This is pretty basic. She had every reason for thinking that her attempt to make her husband emotionally dependent upon her had met with success. Which raises the thorny, complex issue of who is dependent upon and accountable to whom?

Acknowledging that the relationship between money, management and the sexes is not simple and straightforward is not to undermine or dismiss the fundamental fact that women are poor and have little structural power, however. It is not to deny that women perform the emotional labour and that the two facts are connected. But it is to find that not all women are victims. Women do have resources and they can use them; perhaps even more profitably than they presently do. Not all women, of course, are so systematic (some might say cynical) about 'taking out insurance'; just as not all women are so romantic as to do all the emotional work for love. There are many reasons and rationalisations with which women explain their behaviour.

'I do it for a quiet life,' was the response of more than one woman. And another was adamant that her energy went into her husband so as 'to make him fit to live with'. He was a miserable old sod, she said, who would never lift himself out of his own gloom. 'He'd just make my life a misery as well as his own,' Molly said. 'He might look pleasant enough to you, but I'm the one who knows it's not his natural state, I'm the one who knows how much it takes. But if I don't do it, he's just a crank, and I can't live with that.' This was not the only case where a woman claimed the responsibility for a man's mental health. Three women were prepared to take the credit for their husbands' relative sanity. 'Without me to jolly him along and kid him it's all OK,' said one, 'he'd be locked up in no time.'

Women were using their acquired skills to do far more than wheedle money out of men. There were women who were using their skills to ingratiate themselves, to make themselves indispensable and to increase their own importance in a relationship. There were women who were using their energy and expertise to ease some of the pressures on those around them – to reassure, replenish and revitalise. And there were women who were using their resources to establish and maintain a network of relationships on which they themselves could then draw.

So the issue is not whether women do or don't reflect men – or even what form it takes: the issue is whether women are doing it willingly. The dividing line is between the women who said it was their *choice* to boost the egos of men and the women who felt they had no alternative but were forced to follow this pattern of behaviour. Understandably, among the women who saw themselves as being forced, there was a significant number who also saw themselves as exploited.

Most who thought they had to be nice to men were quite explicit in associating their behaviour with fear – they were frightened *not* to. But they were frightened by more than one thing. There were women who expressed their fear of withdrawal of approval and affection ('He won't love me any more'), fear of withdrawal of financial support ('We can't survive without him so I have to keep him any way I can'); and fear of violence. As one woman bluntly said, 'If I don't make him feel good – he beats me.'

Among the women we interviewed were those who said they were forced to please men, to try and 'get on the good side of men', in order to *protect* themselves from rejection, desertion, abuse. But clearly there are no guarantees in this area – given the number of women who testified that they were rejected, neglected or abused – despite all their efforts at emotional management and protection (see Chapter Eight).

Now theoretically it is possible that these women failed to protect themselves because they were not very good at managing men: some women even gave this as the explanation for the way they were treated. One woman in particular considered it to be her fault that her husband was violent. If only she were able to manage better, she said regretfully, he wouldn't be so brutal. We were not so sure: we did not share her framework of analysis.

That the women were not doing enough emotional management – or that what they were doing was not good enough to keep them out of trouble – is one explanation, but it is neither a full nor a satisfactory one. For what has been left out is the possibility that for some men no amount of emotional management would ever be enough to obtain their goodwill or to ensure that they exercise their physical and fiscal power without exploitation.

This is the crux of the business. In the last analysis women are dependent on the goodwill of men. Because men have power and are 'unaccountable' then, no matter what women do, no matter how 'good' women may be, if men do not *want* to behave decently they do not have to: *their* survival is not linked with good behaviour.

This form of sexual inequality has for centuries been a focus for protest for many feminists. Women like the nineteenth-century American historian, Matilda Joslyn Gage, have stated that one of the reasons women are poor and men are rich is precisely because women keep giving all their resources away to men.

While such an explanation is unlikely to figure in a conventional economic analysis, it certainly makes sense within the context of sexual economics. If women are giving up their resources to men and there is *no* reciprocation then clearly the flow is one way. And understandably some can see this as the means whereby men get richer, and women get poorer, every year.

But what *are* these resources that women give away to men? It is one thing to argue that women are placed in a position where they are required to please men, that they engage in emotional management in order to promote the goodwill of men and to protect themselves. It is one thing to argue that women must *trade* with men as a means of existence and in order to survive. But what are the practicalities of this arrangement? What are women actually required to do in the interest of supporting themselves?

When asked what they do to manage men the majority of the women we interviewed gave one short sharp response: sex. Not only was 'sex' seen as something that women should trade in with men, it was also seen as one of the most significant sites of male supremacy. 'The quickest way to a man's pocket is via convincing him of his sexual prowess,' one woman said candidly. 'The more you can convince him he's a great lover, the more he's prepared to pay.' Other women concurred.

Sex was seen as something a woman could give to a man as a token of gratitude, a sign of appreciation. (When we did a reversal and asked, as we consistently did, whether sex was something a man could *give* to a woman we were met with laughter and ridicule: women informed us that men did not *give* sex to women out of appreciation or gratitude but that this was another area where women *give* and men *take*.)

'Sex' was also used by women as a means of gaining the goodwill of men ('I call him Romeo and you can almost see him expand – he thinks I'm great'); it was used to manipulate men ('I pretend that he's the best thing since sliced bread, and he just eats out of my hand') and sex is used to placate and to fend off the wrath of men ('When I see the danger signs I try and get him off to bed and tell him how wonderful he is so he doesn't hit out and sometimes it works').

These were not isolated examples. Distressing and depressing though it may be, many women used sex as a means of defusing the anger and violence of a man: 'It's a bit like a tonic. Every time I see the symptoms I give him a dose. And sometimes it works and all that nastiness goes away. He's back to being healthy and happy in no time.'

It is not surprising that sex should play such a major part in women's management of men for it, too, relates to women's poverty and financial dependence. When men own 99% of the world's wealth and women need some of it, women will trade virtually anything they have got. Currently and historically women have bartered both body and brains in return for board and lodging. Mary Wollstonecraft concluded that there was little to distinguish the women who traded for ready cash with strangers from women who traded with husbands. Her argument caused a furore in the eighteenth century: not only did she insist that wives were legalised prostitutes but also that the ones who were *not* legalised had the better deal.

Her reasons for such an ostensibly outrageous assertion are surprisingly sound. For the legalised prostitute (the wife) had, in Mary Wollstonecraft's terms, less autonomy than her illegal counterpart: not only was the wife prevented from owning property, she had no control over her resources – not even her time – but was supposed to be available to her husband twenty-four hours a day. And she had no guarantee of 'payment' – no guarantee of goodwill or continued support and no protection against redundancy. While not wanting to romanticise prostitution Mary Wollstonecraft did point out that the prostitute had a greater measure of control over her own resources than did the wife.

It was because women were so badly treated within marriage, argued Mary Wollstonecraft, that men found it necessary to deprive women of any other occupation. If there were any alternatives to financial dependence, women would assuredly take them.

This was also the contention of Cicely Hamilton. If women were able to support themselves, she argued, why would they go off and work so hard for men? And she gave new meaning to an old image when she raised the issue of cave man, club in hand, who forcibly dragged off woman to serve him.

Why should woman have gone voluntarily, Cicely Hamilton asks? Does not such unwillingness 'point to a real reluctance to be reduced to permanent servitude on the part of primitive woman – a reluctance understandable enough, since primitive woman's wants being few and easily supplied by herself, there was no need for her to exchange possession of her person for the means of existence' (1909, p.22).

Today, when one can read the words of women such as Mary Wollstonecraft – and Matilda Joslyn Gage, Cicely Hamilton, Rebecca West and Virginia Woolf to name but a select few – it becomes increasingly clear that the problem of women's economic dependence is by no means new. For centuries women have been protesting about the iniquitous financial and social arrangements and there has been consistent and considerable consensus about the extent of the problem, and the nature of the solution.

Underlying both the historical discussion and the contemporary critiques is the premise that men are dominant because men have the money. And along with this insight is the implication that if men did not control the money they would no longer be dominant. While this might be a dismal prospect for some men (and a reason for exercising even tighter control over the wealth) for more than a few women such a possibility is a cause of celebration. For it opens up a whole new possibility for the relationship between the sexes. With men no longer dominant, women would be free to set the terms of their own existence; free even to determine the ways in which they would relate to men. And in such circumstances the world could be a very different place indeed.

Such an assessment of present arrangements and future possibilities is by no means confined to those who profess to be feminists. *Most* women to whom we spoke were of the opinion that when women were financially independent they would be free.

'I'd like to have enough money of my own to be able to tell him what I think of him sometimes,' one woman said. And, 'If women were able to decide about sex, precious little of it there would be,' according to another woman who gave a contemporary analysis of Mary Wollstonecraft's thesis. 'Sometimes I think I'd be better off being a prostitute. At least then I could have a night off – or say time's up. And ask for the money straight. But this way it's sex, sex, sex – every bloody moment of the day it seems to me.'

These were some of the less negative responses. 'If I could earn a decent salary, enough to support me and the children, I'd be off like a shot,' said Melanie. 'But the only way I can keep us is by being nice to him.' The links between economic dependence and 'reflecting men' were painfully clear. The rest of her account suffices to show some of the dimensions of the problem.

'I'd have to say that sex is forced upon me. It's not up to me. I've just got to go through with it. And keep up a good show as well. If I don't – well, he'll look elsewhere. It's that simple. Everyone knows it. But some nights I feel sick when I know what's coming. All day with the kids and then up half the night. The whole thing.

Bright face, lots of smiles, sexy games. Right down to the suspender belt. All the time as though it's the best thing that ever happened to me. And telling him how good he is – what a fantastic lover he makes, which is the biggest lie of all – but what else can I do? I've got four kids. He'd leave. I know he would. So I keep providing exciting sex on demand, I keep him buoyant and feeling good – so that the children and I can eat.'

Melanie did not give the appearance of being pathetic or victimised to the outside world. On the contrary, she looked like a very competent and confident middle-class woman married to an eminently respectable man and surrounded by all the trappings of comfort and security. But she was not at all secure. She was desperate and depressed and she was adamant that economic

dependency was the worst fate there could be. Were there any viable alternative to being supported by a man, she insisted, she would take it.

There were other women, from all walks of life, who were similarly desperate and who also denounced the sexual dimension of dependency upon men. But there were also women who had decided that this was not necessarily a high price to pay.

Nancy, a painter, quite cheerfully stated that she had things pretty well sorted out: 'I look at it this way,' she said, 'I've got a roof over my head, decent food, some money for my art supplies – though I earn most of that myself. But I reckon sex twice a week is no big price to pay for it. And you can't say it takes all that long to keep him happy,' she added with a smile. 'Can't really say it bothers me much. Doesn't turn me on, mind you. And I always plan a few things I'm painting, so it's not exactly time wasted if you know what I mean. And if that's all it takes to keep him in line I can't say I feel badly done by!'

Despite their varied responses, each woman agreed that there were connections between economics and their psychological care of men. In this respect little seems to have changed since Mary Wollstonecraft made her memorable protest against prostitution in 1792. Her famous book, *A Vindication of the Rights of Woman*, was in essence a plea for equal educational and employment opportunities for the sexes, on the grounds that these would lead to the economic equality of the sexes. Yet, while countless women have struggled ever since then to achieve these aims, women are no less dependent on men now than they were before the battle began.

Contemporary feminists are no less caustic than Mary Wollstonecraft was prone to be in their criticisms of the economic and social arrangements which result in women's subordination. While there are some sophisticated economic analyses available (see particularly Barbara Ehrenreich, 1983, and Hilda Scott, 1984) familiarity with their findings is not necessary in order to appreciate some of the fundamentals.

Quite simply, women are poor. They are poor because they are not paid for their work in the home and because they are not paid as well as men when they enter the paid workforce.

This is one of the explanations for the paradoxical facts and figures of the United Nations – that women are working harder, and getting poorer, each year. Clearly women are working harder

– even in western society, where it is now common practice for many women to have not just one job but two. Twenty years ago when women were not expected (or encouraged) to have careers, it was working-class women who were required to do the double shift, who undertook the unpaid work of the home as well as the paid work outside the home. But now the double shift is not confined to working-class women: in the name of liberation and as a measure of progress, most middle-class women have now joined the ranks of those who have two jobs instead of one. This increase in women's work has not brought with it an increase in women's wealth. Although there are no specific figures available for Britain, there is no reason to suspect that they would be dramatically different from the United States where, of all the women between sixteen and sixty-four in the paid work force, 75% cannot support themselves on their income (Hilda Scott, 1984, p.17).

This paradox is easily explained: women do more work than men but some of it is unpaid and most of it for less pay than men. While the percentage varies in different western countries it generally hovers around the two-thirds mark with women in Britain currently earning about 65% of the men's rate of pay and women in the United States slightly less. Add to this the fact that more women than men provide the sole support for their families and some of the contributing causes of women's poverty are uncovered.

Such a problem should not be impossible to solve. If women were to be paid – *properly* – for their work, they would soon cease to be poor. Women would start to accumulate their own resources and this would lead to autonomy – to economic and psychological independence. This is the reasoning behind such current campaigns as Wages for Housework: it was the reasoning in the past behind everything from the demand for family allowance and child endowment to the nineteenth-century feminist struggle for equal educational opportunity. Pay women, and not just men, for their work and there will soon be sexual equality – or so the supporters of this stand suggest.

But such an achievement seems as unattainable now as it did centuries ago when the sights were first set. This is partly because, as economists have so ably demonstrated, no country could afford to pay for the work of women at the same rate as that paid to men. In 1972 the Chase Manhattan National Bank conducted a survey of women's work in the United States, and concluded that if all unpaid housework had been paid for at the going rate for the job, 'it would have cost twice the national budget' (Hilda Scott, 1984, p.60).

This does not mean, however, that men should be paid while women's labour is unrewarded. It would be a more equitable arrangement if women were paid more and men were paid less, but such provision seems to hold little appeal for men and represents something of a social problem, to say the least. For while there is nothing new in the philosophy of taking from the rich and giving to the poor, it is not one that has proved to be wildly popular among the rich. And because it is men who are in charge of the wealth, it would be men who would have to decide to redistribute the resources. Which is why things will probably remain as they are: with men relatively rich and with women continuing to be poor.

Economic theory does not present the plight of women in these terms. Economists have shown no desire to examine the commerce between the sexes; they have neither analysed women's work in general nor considered the specifically female task of reflecting men. There is little discussion on the dimensions of women's dependency or on its repercussions. Instead, the discipline of economics itself has made a most significant and legitimating contribution to financial inequality by passing off as *natural* the practice of paying men more than women.

At the core of economic theory is the assumption that women are supported by men. This simple assumption helps to construct the vicious circle of women's dependence. When economists, and the members of society, assume that women are supported by men, then it is perfectly logical to put the case that women do not need as much money as men.

And what happens when it is believed that women do not need as much money as men? Why, then they are not paid for their work, or they are paid less than men.

And what happens when women are not paid as much as men? Why, they must turn to men for support.

And what happens when women turn to men for support? They stop pleasing themselves and start to please men. They flutter around, flatter and try to find favour.

And what happens when women make men the centre of attention and place their physical and psychological resources at the service of men? The flow of resources and wealth goes one way, from women to men. If there is no reciprocation, then the harder women work the richer men get. By such means, male supremacy becomes a reality.

Adrienne Rich (1981) is one of the latest in a long line of feminists to spell out the implications of these sexual economics. Taking up where Cicely Hamilton and Rebecca West left off, Adrienne Rich argues that women are being driven into the arms of men, whether or not that is where they want to be. And she does not call this legalised prostitution but 'compulsory hetero-sexuality', maintaining that when the system has been designed so that women must have men in order to meet their economic needs, then men are a necessity, they are a compulsory item, and heterosexuality hardly qualifies as a 'preference'.

From famous feminists to hassled housewives, it is widely accepted that it is the economic dependency of women which is at the crux of sexual inequality. Implicitly and explicitly most of the women to whom we spoke acknowledged that the thread of women's financial dependency and *absence of choice* runs through everything from the way women boost the egos of men to the nature of women's sexual relationships with men.

Over the centuries, debates on the origins of women's sub-ordination have been varied and virulent. Explanations have ranged from nature to nurture, from individual to social responsi-bility, and yet all that can be claimed with certainty is that it is not known – and probably never can be known – how it all started. Although it is not necessary to know how the subordination of women began in order to know how to end it, it can be useful to have some idea of how far women are voluntarily entering the present arrangements which appear to disadvantage them. Do women jump or are they pushed?

We had concluded that women were primarily pushed. That women were managing men because they were financially de-pendent and there was little else they could do. We would have been among the first to admit that this was not always a bad thing. Enough women had told us they thought the arrangement was fair – and enough had indicated that they derived enjoyment from their bolstering of men – for us to appreciate that this was not a demanded and demeaning task for every woman. But we were still reasonably convinced that these women were the lucky ones: they were fortunate to have been able to make 'a good deal' within a system which was not of their choice. And we were reasonably convinced that if women did have a choice they would soon set up a very different system. However, Rosemary did not share our conviction.

An official in an Australian teachers' union, a feminist firmly committed to financial independence for women, Rosemary had little faith in women's economic future. Her personal experience had caused her to doubt women's capacity not just to attain economic independence but to sustain it, once achieved. In Rosemary's opinion, it was not that women had their resources taken from them – it was that women were giving them away.

'If all women were given one hundred thousand pounds tomorrow,' one woman said to Rosemary, 'the day afterwards just about every supposedly "happy couple" we know now would cease to exist.'

Rosemary could not agree: 'Rubbish,' she replied. 'If all women were given one hundred thousand pounds tomorrow – the day afterwards most of them would give it to their husbands.'

The context was a restaurant in Australia: the company was comprised predominantly of women with careers who were capable of supporting themselves; the conversation was heated; but at the centre was the old chicken-and-egg debate.

Three women (interviewer included initially) were arguing that it was because women were economically dependent that women reflected men: one woman, Rosemary, insisted that it was the other way around, that it was because women reflected men, because women gave away all their resources to men that women were poor and had to be supported by men.

'I should know,' Rosemary said, 'I see it happen all the time. All these women teachers who are financially independent. And what do they do with it? Have it paid into their husband's bank accounts. Give it away to men. Just hand over their financial independence.' To a chorus of disapproval she declared that such women did not deserve to be paid decent salaries.

The atmosphere was electric. Cora was outraged: 'I'm one of the women you are talking about! I'm one of the dreadful women who has my salary paid into my husband's bank account, damn you,' she exploded. 'And why? Why? Why do you think I do it? Because it's less work, that's why. Because it's easier . . . If I had more money than my husband do you know how long it would take me to make him feel important?' she demanded to know. 'Do you know how much time and energy I'd have to spend trying to convince him he's a real man? There just wouldn't be enough hours in the day,' she said flatly. 'So I let him appear big. It's the only way I can have any life of my own.'

Unlike the many women who had informed us that because they were financially dependent they were psychologically (or physically) exploited, Cora was saying that she *bought* her psychological autonomy by handing over her paypacket! Her rationale was straightforward and sound. Not only did it take no effort on her part to have her money paid to her husband, but it left her emotionally free: given financial control he was confident, content and required very little ego-boosting.

'He always gives me money when I ask for it,' Cora explained. 'In fact he likes me to ask for it and likes to look generous. It isn't as if I don't have access to it, or that he keeps me poor.' And she went on to explain how important it was for her husband to be seen to be in charge of the money – to 'wear the trousers' – and to sustain the myth of male dominance.

While, in the course of the discussion, Rosemary qualified some of her assertions and admitted that the practice might not be as simple as it seemed (she acknowledged that there could be extenuating circumstances, that women could *use* the system and were not necessarily always used by it), she would not abandon her analysis. It was still her contention that women would reflect men even when they were not economically dependent on men.

And three women sat and weighed the pros and cons of the way women in top jobs (or the very few that they knew) felt obliged to boost the deflated egos of their male subordinates. They even decided that the further up the career ladder women moved, the more likely they were to assuage the fears of the men around them: there seemed to be an inverse correlation in that the *less* they relied on the men, the *more* time they spent in making them feel good.

'Look at Jessie,' Rosemary said, referring to a high-flyer in the civil service. 'She doesn't need those guys for anything. She doesn't depend on them for money, for love – not even for approval. She's their boss and her job's absolutely secure. And so what does she do? She spends half her working time making them feel good. Why? She calls it good management: I call it being a wimp!'

Although Rosemary's is not an attractive explanation (and has connotations of blaming the victim) it does have distinct advantages. For if the whole structure of sexual inequality depends simply upon women being wimps, then the whole structure of sexual inequality could collapse if and when women cease to be wimps. This is the basis of Germaine Greer's thesis: she has argued that women have given up their resources to men and that it is high time they took them back and used them for themselves. She has said that it is within the power of every woman to define her own boundaries, to set herself at the centre of the universe, to 'husband' her own resources and to relate to men from a position of strength. In fact, *The Female Eunuch* (1970) and *Sex and Destiny* (1984) are based on the philosophy that women can claim their autonomy and that they don't need to be paid one hundred thousand pounds tomorrow in order to start. Germaine Greer has insisted that it is the right and the responsibility of every woman to start saying what she thinks, instead of saying what she thinks men want to hear. And if and when *all* women realise their independence then the revolution will have been completed.

While women themselves have suggested that it might not be so simple, while they have revealed that there are as many 'good' reasons for reflecting men as for not doing so, and while it is impossible to arrive at a simple analysis and a straightforward solution to this problem, there is one 'truth' which seems to have emerged and which remains unchallenged. It is that while ever women continue to give away their resources to men, while ever women nurture and manage men and there is *no* reciprocation, then the flow of resources will be one way. Women will continue to be subordinate, dependent, poor and open to exploitation.

In the interest of ending oppression and of redistributing the world's resources, Karl Marx once made the seemingly simple suggestion that the workers of the world should unite. On the comparable grounds that it would end oppression and result in a more equitable allocation of the world's wealth, perhaps women should be urged to adopt a suitable and similar strategy: perhaps the recommendation to women should be that they should refuse to reflect men.

7

HARMONY IN THE HOME

'We have a very close and very happy family. And it doesn't just happen that way. I count it as *my* achievement. I made it happen. I've "managed" my husband – as you put it – for our entire married life. Almost fifty years. And it's been worth it.'

Florence saw her 'happy family' very much as her own creation. And she genuinely believed that one of the most important things in life was the security and support which comes from such a family. From the account she gave of her husband, children and grandchildren there emerged an advertisement for all that is best in the nuclear family.

It was not that Florence was sentimental. On the contrary, she acknowledged how much work had gone into her creation, how frustrating it had been on occasion and how frequently she had had to keep a tight rein on her own feelings and fears, for the sake of the family. She emphasised the daily and invisible work which goes into fostering and maintaining the dynamics of family relationships. But, as she said, although there had been times when she had asked herself whether it was all worth it, she now looked at her family and knew that, in her case, she had obtained more than her just reward.

Interestingly, Florence did not think that it was possible for women today to do what she had done. She pointed out that fifty years ago, when she had married, it was acceptable – even desirable – for a woman to have no aspirations for paid work but to devote herself to her family. She assured us that it had not looked like self-sacrifice. According to Florence, husbands then had been much more conscious of how much they needed wives and although each sex did very different jobs, as far as she was concerned there had been mutual respect.

She did not think that she had worked harder than her husband in those early years of marriage, and she knew that her days were frequently more pleasant than his. She was content to rear her children; she had found it positively enjoyable and exhilarating to provide them with a stimulating pre-school environment. There had been no money but she had had enormous fun entertaining the children. It had been a satisfying life and both her husband and society had valued what she was doing.

There had been nothing unfair about the help she had given her husband in his career. It had seemed that the least she could do was to build up his confidence and to relieve him of every responsibility so that at night he was free to study. It had seemed only sensible to put concern for his work and promotion at the centre of family consideration and to keep the children quiet. And when she realised she could help in more practical ways she was pleased to be able to read some of his texts and make summaries for him – although, as she said with sardonic humour, she had never made the mistake of appearing to know more than he did, even though she had been reasonably confident *she* would have done very well in his exams. But she felt no resentment at all, even though her husband has achieved some public recognition while she remained the wife in the wings. She knew that he had appreciated her efforts and that the whole family had benefited from his small success.

After the children were 'off her hands' Florence had worked in her husband's business but now they had both retired and she was more than satisfied with their life together. They were an elderly couple, she said, who still preferred each other's company to anyone else's, who took great joy in their family and who had experienced the best that life had to offer. She defied anyone to state that her life had been wasted.

'I didn't sacrifice myself when I got married. I didn't see it as demeaning to put my husband first, to make him happy, to wait on him or make the home revolve around him. I saw the creation of a happy family as a real challenge. It took hard work, under-standing, management – even "flair" – to keep five human beings happy under the one roof. I felt I was good at my job and I took pride in it. I knew the key to a happy family was managing the man and not for a minute do I regret doing it. I would do it all again – except I don't think it's possible today.'

One of the reasons Florence believed it wasn't possible for women today to live as she had done was because of the experience of her daughters. Both had been divorced and had enjoyed her full support. With a new twist to the old idea of 'progress' she declared that her daughters had not had the fair deal which had fallen to her in life. Despite the fact that both had had paid work throughout their marriages, she firmly believed that they had been required to be 'doormats' in a way that she had not.

No credence was given to their role in creating 'a family', she said. It wasn't just a biological unit: a family was an emotional unit and yet neither society, nor the husbands, had ever acknowledged the work that her daughters had done to create harmonious family relationships. Women now were so often rated according to their paid work (and they didn't seem to rate at all if they didn't have any) and yet there was no one to support women in *their* jobs, as women still supported men.

'I would have been at home all day, but when my husband got in he was just as interested in *my* day as I was in *his*. Not like it was for my daughter,' Florence said disgustedly. 'I'd watch her rushing in from work having collected the children, negotiated with the child minder, done the shopping. She'd be sorting clothes with one hand and getting the supper with the other while she tried to talk to the children about their day. And then in would come her husband and everything had to be for him. His day. His problems. And why wasn't there a bit of order about the place? He'd take himself off with a drink – "to relax" – and she'd have to fuss around him. I used to think if my daughter had been a servant she would have been treated better. I'd get hopping mad about it.

'So it wasn't such a shock when one day my daughter just broke down and said it was all too much. I could see it coming. I knew something had to go. And I knew who I thought was the biggest problem. I told her. Her life is much easier now she's divorced. Not financially of course. We try to help her all we can. But it's easier as a family. In fact, now she's divorced I think she and the children really are a "happy family". A thriving "unit". They weren't while she was married.'

We have quoted Florence at length because of the many interesting issues that her account raises. Is women's emotional management of men different now from what it has been in the past? Men may not have reciprocated in kind in former times, but according to Florence's view they did reciprocate. Could it be that what was once a real and valued contribution from women has now become an unfair and unacknowledged burden? Such an explanation would fit in with the findings on women and poverty and would justify Florence's rather unusual stand of defending her own management of a man while declaring that this was an impossible task for her daughters.

Now in a position to reflect on the decisions she had made, Florence provided a very different picture of male-ego management from some of the younger women who were still in the process of making, and weighing up, their decisions about family relationships. And there were other women of Florence's generation who shared her perspective on 'husbands first'. But they believed this was a matter of necessity, and not choice. Whereas Florence had seen her creation of a thriving emotional family unit as an achievement, they looked back over their lives and experienced the management of their husbands' egos as an acute personal loss for themselves.

We spoke to two more women, Doris aged seventy-one, and Nancy-Amelia aged sixty-two, both 'strong-minded old war horses' as Doris put it. Like Florence, they both saw themselves as members of the 'old school of husband managers' (Nancy-Amelia's phrase) whose reliance on emotional service is part of a tradition of home, family, and menfolk first, which they believe is neither emulated nor sought after by today's younger women. Where they differed sharply, and significantly, from Florence, was that in both their cases, they recognised that devoting themselves to their men's management for the sake of a happy home had severely disadvantaged their own intellectual development and personal fulfilment.

Unusually for middle-class women of working-class origins (both had been 'factory gels', one in Cardiff, the other in Bristol), they had both decided to abandon (temporarily) the mixed blessing of looking up to and after their husbands, in order to, as Nancy-Amelia put it, 'better oneself and give woman's soul a chance'. The chance came for each of them at a local night school: Doris was sixty-seven years old, living in Bristol; Nancy-Amelia was forty-eight and living in Cardiff. Both women were excited, moved and politically and emotionally changed by their first flirtation with education and a life outside their traditional, domestic role. They both found enormous satisfaction from their evening classes. In both cases, however, this led to dissatisfaction, conflicts and problems with their husbands.

Doris's adventure lasted for one year. It resulted in her gaining her first O level at age sixty-eight years and an upsurge of pride and confidence in herself. It was followed almost immediately by a decision to return to her former domestic life.

'I suppose I was always competent and able at everything I turned my hand to. But none of us girls ever had any education. Some of us went into a cigarette factory, the rest of us were shooed off into undies. At fourteen I was a seamstress in a bras and corsets factory. All of us girls, (seven in our family, there were) were always told a woman's job is to give in to your man, always be inclined to agree, never have a confrontation, walk away if necessary, come back with a smile on your face and a good bread and butter "pud" for his tea. I always carried on like that, and it definitely worked right with Ben. He was very good to me and our children. If I took something up and he didn't like it, I knew it was best to give it up. My old nan had taught us girls to put our backs into our homes and value peace and a quiet life.'

Doris stuck to these values throughout her marriage to Ben, a 'decent straightforward man who would always protect his family and keep them well fed and clothed'. She excelled at every kind of cooking, sewing, embroidery and handicraft and she explained: 'Ben never minded me popping off to those classes. After all, everything I learnt there could be put to use in our lovely home. We were all more comfortable when I enlarged my skills in those ways.'

She admits that her sharp mind made her intensely competitive and she sometimes had difficulty curbing her aggressive spirit. 'I had to content myself with mammoth crosswords, and powerful games of Scrabble and watching Mastermind. I'd even have to play myself down there, and let Ben win occasionally. He never wanted me to use my brains in any formal way. Instead we took up bridge and ballroom dancing which we could do as a couple. Nothing competitive.'

However, in the later years of their marriage Ben became ill and there was less they were able to do together. Doris grew restless; one day a young friend of her son's invited her to join his politics class in the city. 'Ben was against it from the first but finally I persuaded him. Well, how I enjoyed that class! It woke up my addled old brain, gave me loads to think about. But the kind of discussion it provoked at home certainly didn't help towards a peaceful life! Ben got furious at my new opinions, often quite different from his. He even objected to my right to hold such opinions, the more so as I was now able to back them up.

'My homework and reading meant we had less elaborate meals, fewer quiet games of Scrabble. I was sometimes invited out by other members of the class and that didn't go down too well. All in all, it was very upsetting to the harmony of the home.

'I began to take less pleasure in the studies. However, I worked very hard, took the exam, and was overjoyed at nearly seventy to get an O level. But when I broke the news to my son and husband they weren't impressed, indeed they hardly seemed interested. It was as if I'd done nothing important, just as usual. If anything they rather ignored my Big News. It was nothing to make a fuss about, they seemed to be saying. You can imagine how that took the edge off my excitement.

'After that I had a long hard think. I'd spent years helping to build a home with warmth and affection in it, and now there was tension and difficulties. Just because I had stepped outside my role. Well, I couldn't let it all go wrong now, particularly as Ben was very ill. Conflict was out of the question. Ben wasn't a demonstrative man. He never talked things over with me the way young people do today. That wasn't the old style of achieving happiness. More's the pity!

'But he was stern, good and honest and did the right things by his lights. All he asked in return was that I devoted myself to him and family life and allowed him, where he thought proper, the last word on everything.'

Doris felt that because Ben was unable to encourage her new interests he needed her constant protection in order for the marriage to survive. 'We are not as young as we were so I shall bite my tongue, button my mouth, and bide my time.'

Doris's story is sad, but it is not atypical. Quite a few women of her generation expressed regret at the lost opportunities; 'lost' not because they were technically unavailable, but because the women could not have availed themselves of the opportunities without jeopardizing their marriages.

Nancy-Amelia Garnett (Auld NAG to her friends) is one woman who explicitly stated her regrets. A remarkable woman by any standards, her story (which we quote at length and with the aid of some of her letters) helps to reveal the price women pay for preserving harmony in the home.

NAG's 'little flurry of self-interest' which lasted for nine years, began after thirty years of pampering Henry, her 'Old Man', but it was temporary. Like Doris, she decided that she eventually had to return to a domestic life. She did not want to but there was no choice.

When she first started on her path to 'growth and develop-ment', her Old Man was on the assembly line in a large Cardiff factory and about to be promoted. Nancy-Amelia, who had no formal qualifications of any sort, was a 'very genteel seamstress and sales assistant' in a large Cardiff dress and underwear store 'where we catered for some lovely larger ladies'.

Nancy-Amelia tended her garden, read avidly, sewed ex-quisitely, shyly composed verse and painted delicate water-colours. One day she saw an advertisement for a child care certified course at the local technical college. 'It was only for a year,' she told us. 'Suddenly the Auld NAG got the bit between her teeth. I was nearly fifty and I knew if I didn't seize my chance then I never would. Fortunately, it wasn't too hard to win the Old Man round. Not that time!'

Nancy-Amelia Garnett spent the next nine years winning the Old Man round while she sat for and passed her child care certificate, eight O levels, three A levels, a degree in arts from Cardiff University and, finally, a postgraduate certificate in education. When that was completed and her sparkling back kitchen glistened with hard-won trophies, in a town that was a bastion of unemployment, where young highly qualified middle-class male graduates could not find work, Nancy-Amelia held down two major teaching jobs while she was, as she says proudly, 'almost at pensionable age'.

Over the years her tutors and lecturers have praised her talent and ability. She became an expert in sculpture and fine art, displayed skills in literary appreciation and criticism, showed an unusual talent for dramatic art and creative writing and exhibited unusual capabilities for sociological and philosophical analysis. It seemed that there was nothing at which she could not excel. She was content: 'My soul drank it all in. I was thirsty for knowledge. I felt blissful reading and learning. I grew proud of myself as a woman.'

Only one thing remained out of her reach: a way of combining personal fulfilment with domestic harmony.

'Managing menfolk is a matter of survival,' she said. 'If the Old Man and I were to survive together I had to keep acting the same way me mam did. But the more I learnt the harder it became.'

Finally, she settled back into family life. Over the following turbulent years she kept in touch with one of the authors, her former tutor. These few extracts from the Auld NAG's letters (with her permission) chart her problems and progress better than modest Nancy-Amelia could be prevailed upon to do.

During her O level course

'I am writing dear friend to thank you for the leather volume of our mutual friend Will. Why doesn't everyone read Shakespeare? He is truly amazing. Will you come to tea with the dear Old Man and my poor self? The Young Man may also be visiting that weekend so it will be best not to bring up anything contentious. Although the child care certificate was fun and enormously satisfying to one's womanly spirit, these new O levels are joyous. So many things to find out, though all that woman's role stuff you have been preaching is creating some havoc with the OM. I shall, of course, have your favourite cakes baked . . .'

Second year O level course

'I write dear friend to tell you how exciting the whole group found the drama presentation of the Suffragettes. I don't think any of us had understood about the hunger strikes or what they stood for. I myself have never felt prouder than playing Lady Constance Lytton. Knowing her innermost feelings as I surely do now, I have to say she is just simply Dame Connie to me! I felt quite shivery as I knew I (or rather Connie) was about to throw that stone at Mr Lloyd George's car. Oh, how moving I found her words as she shouted: "How can you, who say you back the women's cause, stay on in a government which refuses them the vote and is persecuting them for asking for it?"*

'I am glad we all did you credit. Of course, when I tried to relive some of the thrills for the OM it all fell rather flat. Decent and

---

* Midge Mackenzie, 1975: 133.

upstanding as he is, he is still filled with pomp and circumstance and has to be in the right and does not appreciate our Cause at all. It made me very sad.

'The Young Man is back again at home for a while and living between the two of them is like living between two fires. Talk about role conflict. Button your lips, Auld NAG, I say every morning. If you can no longer say what they want to hear best to stay mum.'

Holidays between O level and A level

'I have no doubt but that I want to continue. But it is somewhat of a hard life at present. How naive I used to be. Why didn't you tell me in a stronger language what a spoiled and cosy comfortable creature I was? I am filled with awareness of what I have gained . . . it is a great deal, and gratitude truly pours from me . . . but I am also becoming bitterly aware that some things have gone for ever, including many of the simple comforts and much of the cosiness. No, I am not unhappy, but yes, there is a certain loneliness. I do not find too much to talk of to the family or those old acquaintances, and with you and the others soon to move away, I fear the shared experiences may have to be borne alone. Take care of your good self . . .'

During her A level course

'The beauty of poetry and art is almost too much for my soul to stand. There is a kind of magic to education and thought, like walking through pine forests in France; which ordinary people, and particularly ordinary women like myself, are seldom allowed to experience.'

After obtaining her A level certificate

'Well who's the lucky Auld NAG! Yes I feel good about it, though it is a hard life and that last term was the hardest of the lot and many's the time I felt like throwing it all up, and I don't just mean academics. I want to carry on, but life on the home front, folks, is very edgy nowadays. I have too many new wonderful women and men to look up to and learn from, to be giving my *all* to my devoted old sod. It is hard to be free of soul in deepest suburbia, getting the OM's tea and telling him how great he is. But he has a poor life the dear wretch, so I keep those feelings on a tight rein. Just the odd sneaky look at my mounting certificates, tending the garden, breathing in God's good air and wishing it were enough to comfort me with my women's conflicts, and writing the odd long letter. To do any hard grind I now have to get up at 5.00 am to have it all neatly put away so as not to cause any rows when he rises.'

On holiday after A level
before she makes the decision to go to university

'The sea is calm tonight and so is the Auld NAG. I wish I had brought along my poetry or women's fiction books, but thought it best to have a holiday without trouble. As I watch the Old Atlantic showing most of her moods, she is so beautiful, tears rise at the grandeur of sight and sound. I remember our old mate Matthew [Arnold] and how he always put my jumbled feelings into words. I sometimes speculate whether he and my tired old bedfellow would have got on. You would say yes because they are both chauvinists! The OM certainly is, but we are a little easier now with that course behind me and both of us less tired. I do not know if I dare continue. The OM has such a wretched job and needs my support all of the time. Role conflict, role conflict that's what I keep saying to myself. Some days, pal, I wish I'd never heard that word. Some days I wonder, was I happier before you helped me on these terrible but beautiful journeys? I don't really mean that. Have a good holiday yourself . . .'

The university: year one

'I feel damn lucky to have broken free of the tweed coat and shopping basket brigade which is the female norm down our way. Many's the day I speak my mind. Far too many, the OM says. He is getting very upset these days. Home has its dreadful rough patches. It isn't fair is it? I was truly glad to get off on the holidays as sewing had piled up and household chores stared meekly at me, while I had a touch of the Hamlets.'

Holidays after year one

'The OM and I are well, though not ecstatic if you know what I mean. The Young Man visits often and there are big rows. Both my beloveds send you their greetings. I feel bitter that Henry deserves better than his futile boring job and can do little about it. It is no wonder he feels he deserves a flattering loving wife, which nowadays he doesn't often get. Can it be that soon I am to receive my free bus pass? Which shows how the years pass, and so many spent nurturing him. It should not be a lot to ask of a woman, but God knows it is.

'Now to your crucial questions. Will I go back? Well, why pal do I want more? I suppose almost because it isn't heaven on the home front and it ought to be. The OM and I are more even-stevens now, not that we will ever have an equal partnership, that is not to be, not anyway if we want a happy home. But I know I have more bargaining than before. It isn't easy. Well, was it ever?'

The university: year two

'The penny has at last dropped and I have become a horrible person and often won't lift a finger, there being two of us who could undertake the chores.

'I often think of the good times and Dame Connie and her stone. Wasn't that sure something to be proud of? I guess I know where to throw my stone if I had one . . .'

Holidays: after year two at university

'I am trying to enjoy leading a wifely lifestyle with some trimmings, like watching Robert Redford on the television. Of course, I could piss off to the South of France and be a governess and find me a gigolo. The great thing is I now know I can choose.

'I am still placing white, purple and green flowers and plants around the house whenever the male chauvinism gets too much. It gives me something to hang on to.

'Apart from the set-tos on the home front all goes well and I still love the studying. No, I haven't made many friends at college. Some are younger than I am, and in general it is best not to, for reasons you will understand.'

Third year university

'You will be glad to know I am at last liberated from the longing for love and approval from the two men in my family. But the OM and I are on another no-speak, no-touch, soul-destroying spell, which at one time would almost have broken my heart. Now I'm happy to say I can handle it with calm and spunk. This time I would not give in and agree. I would not doff my cap. I absolutely refused. (Am I a nasty old NAG?) So finally the Old Man cracked and came home with a bottle of sherry for me. Alas, I've been too cheaply bought over, and brought round, for too many years. It will take more than a bottle of plonk this time. I still love the Old Fellow. He is a decent guy and none kinder when he gets his own way, but I am a big girl now and no mere female cap-doffer.'

Nancy-Amelia Garnett gets her degree

'I went down to the University this morning and what do you think I saw? "Successful candidate Nancy-Amelia Garnett, BA." Well, it is only an Ordinary Degree, dear teacher and friend, but it isn't ordinary to me. I was fully stretched to pass and damned lucky to make it. But it is a bit of a pyrric (perric? pyryc?) victory, and I am more like a damp squib as troubles with the OM loom large. In his opinion I am getting increasingly uppity and a trial to live with, and he says in others' opinions also. Our home and family are often unhappy. Everything I do is wrong.

'I feel a failure as a parent and as a wife. BUT A GREAT BLOODY SUCCESS AS AN ALMOST EMANCIPATED DAME!

'The sagging chest was lifted and the head stood high as the Auld NAG descended the steps of the University (a third-rate building I must say!) to see her name posted. What would they say in Ladies Lingerie and Larger Fittings now?

'I bought half a bottle of Moët et Chandon to drink on my own this afternoon, there being no one in Cardiff who would understand my true feelings. Then better nature overcame me and wouldn't allow me to drink it without sharing it with the old fellow. God knows he neither understands nor appreciates the nature of the victory (and between us he hasn't exactly contributed to its success) nor does he even like champagne.

'Must close now as the OM is at the door and the tea is not prepared and there will be another row, especially as I have had my curls cut off. My hair has been cut short in chunks, very trendy as the Young Man's girlfriend would say, but then the Auld NAG is not so young any more and these things are not allowed.'

Holidays after university: uncertain whether to do teacher training

'All is over for a while. I am ready for a brief respite from the rat race. Back to the safety of home. No, it hasn't been easy. But at last I think I have no more tears to shed. The well has dried up. At least I can now tackle the home front from a stronger position, with more balanced judgement, without overdue care for what the world thinks about me and mine.

'I have had my time and now I am back to managing man and home, though cap-doffing somedays sticks in my throat. However, my flowers grow sweetly perfumed and it will work out.

'At least the OM is reliable and the YM basically decent and God knows I appreciate them both, and still sometimes blush and get in a flurry of excitement when either of them has been away and returns to my arms, which is how it should be. But still they cannot appreciate any of the new ideas I believe in. (Of course, if the analysis put forward by these ideas is correct, how can they?)

'We had one of our terrible Air Clearers earlier this week and they blamed everything on my education and not a little on women's rights. I stood up for myself and told them how obnoxious it was to have two bloody self-righteous men in the house to wait on and serve all the time. But this kind of upset is not good for family life. So I shall have to return to my secret flurries and in public back to the building up . . .'

Nancy-Amelia goes to college for a postgraduate teaching certificate

'The OM is away for a few days which is good as I am in the middle of what is already a sixteen-page essay. Best to get it over in his absence. I have so much homework, like never before, that once again I have left the chores so you know what that means . . . It does seem a shame to hurry it, I hear you say. No, not the housework, the essay. Yes, I agree, but things being as they are (not to say worse) it is the best thing to do.

'As it was, before the OM left, I let our braised steak burn whilst composing pages five and six, but what the hell, nowadays I know it is not the end of the world. But I can't tell the old fellow that. Too many rumpuses as it is.'

Teaching practice

'Teaching practice is without doubt the hardest hurdle yet. How do teachers survive? Staff rooms are funny places. Some I really hate. But many are better than the scenes in our back kitchen at present and I struggle on.

'I do feel very useful. It is a full timetable and with things blowing up at home I may only manage this cert. ed. lark by the skin of my teeth. Of course, there is the chance I may not manage it, and I hate to let everyone down.

'The head teacher in the school I attend is a lot like my sister so I do not always know which way the wind blows. What with that, and Henry blowing cold more often than hot, there have been chilly days at school and chilly nights at home. So it is good to have some memories to warm oneself by.

'As I am on a three-week block practice, and the OM is bedridden with his back, I have had to return to the 5 am schedule, it being the only way to fulfil all of one's duties. I pray God will help me to get through this hard time.'

Nancy-Amelia passes her postgraduate certificate of education

'Although it is just like a miracle that I have somehow passed this gruelling test which was ten times more difficult than anything I have attempted before, I do not think I can continue with this learning/teaching lark. Academic rewards as well, you know, bring one a very gruelling time at home.

'My lovely lady supervisor tells me if I do not work in an infant classroom it will be criminal as I am above average as an infant teacher so thank you for giving me the encouragement that began this carry-on.

'Two other lecturers, one being my tutor, say I could also teach young, out-of-work adults, returning to learn in this sad city, as I have a "good way" with basic learners. How strange of them not to realise that it's because I am one myself. It is difficult to know what to do.

'I just want you to be assured I am my own woman and walk a little bit taller and have a lot less to say and a lot more to think. The words have great magic. It is a good feeling. One I never could have imagined in my days in the factory or even later in the shop. There are many with bad natures who say I am too old to keep it up now. Most of them are young and male. You will not be surprised. Anyway, here's hoping, but here's wondering.

'As you know, the home front and my dear ones are precious. So it may be that yours truly is finally out to graze.'

Nancy-Amelia takes her first teaching post

'This is a very poor area of what you used to call downtown Cardiff. The poor folk I teach are decent intelligent boys and girls, but the teachers who have been paid for sixteen years to educate them, have on the larger scale only served to oppress, suppress and intimidate the majority of them. Specially the poor girls. Some are so meek it pains me. I won't have it go on. Like you once said we are in the business of "confidence-making" and it is great to see results.

'But back on the home front, little boosts my own confidence and I have to take special pains to uplift theirs. Yes, I still do it because I feel for the OM with his miserable existence, and the YM with his family troubles and bringing up his child on his own (of course, I know women do it all the time). I have to say there is more trouble than there was.

'I do not think we shall be able to come and visit this year but you are very much in my thoughts.'

Nancy-Amelia gives up her job

'Sorry to have been such a bad correspondent. I have not worked these last months and am still very tired. It all got too much. Now I walk every week to the unemployment office to sign on, and am exhausted. Am also in the middle of menopausal miseries when one's blood feels like hot and gritty sand. I recall you laughing and saying the menopause is a male myth. Well, dear teacher, you are wrong, for misery there is. Wait till the hormones catch up with you!'

Nancy-Amelia offered a job

'They rang for me again to go back to work. They feel I have something to offer young people. It is precious to hear. But I cannot make up my mind. I struggle this way and that. The education lark makes me less able to give enough time and attention to family life. I stand up for myself too much and give cheek where I never would before. This kind of going-on cuts into the old values. I do not think I shall return.'

Offered another job a few months later

'I was offered that job again. Some young people still ask after me. When I reckoned it up I decided it wasn't worth it. Biting the tongue gets harder when you are your own self and valued in the outside world. So I content myself in the garden. Strangely, the suffragette borders, although they flower the correct mauve and white, are now springing some yellow! What does this off-colour note tell us? I see friends and relatives, get the OM his usual breakfast at six-thirty, such things have their own old-fashioned pleasures. He has a wearisome life poor sod, has not had my blessed opportunities, but must stick with the daily grind. You would be glad to hear he is changing a great deal. We have many reasonable conversations, and he washes up frequently.'

Nancy-Amelia reconsiders and returns to work

'You will be glad to know the old warhorse is in harness again. With a full wage-packet I feel almost like a real person. I know working makes me selfish, too much my own self, not enough the little wife. Being self-centred does not go down well in the back kitchen of Laurel Lane. But it is something to help feed and clothe us and our lovely ones. That makes me proud. I am a big girl now, so well educated. The long trek has been worthwhile. I can think and act for myself in the ways I always should have done. But still I don't want to push that fact up the old man's nose as it does not make for pleasant living. It is still better that he thinks he is the boss and knows more than I do which is becoming harder. There are few perks in the old sod's working life so it is more than ever up to me to make him comfortable. That and teaching leaves one quite knackered.'

Nancy-Amelia gives up work

'You were with us in thought yesterday; first, when the BBC did a programme on Auden; secondly, when they had some radical stuff on Women's Hour. Well, perhaps not very radical, but in this most dutiful and wifely existence every crumb counts.

'It has been as you know a year of funerals and sadnesses and the terrible tragedy of the YM's wee one is with us still. Any provocation on my part would have been cruel.

'Of course, I miss many things about the job, but it was very tiring. I know I am a nasty cow at times but I also realise I am a sheet anchor to this family in their times of need, and perhaps it was wrong to shut myself off from them and stick up so many times for myself.

'When things get bad I take a good shot of whisky and think of pals like Keats and Browning and your favourite Lizzie Browning. You are right about there not being sufficient women poets on my shelf, but at college they are largely ignored or put-down . . . so what is new? Thoughts like that are the sort that bring sparks into household discussions.

'We have had a couple of major set-tos so it is best for the moment not to include me in anything you plan, like that research you mentioned. It would not help anything this end.'

Christmas: Nancy-Amelia still unemployed

'Your unexpected visit was certainly a wonderful event. How little you have changed. The Old Man thoroughly enjoyed your visit too. He said he was quite exhilarated by the usual sparring with you!

'Thank you for the mountain of books and papers. We have little money for luxuries like that. Winter approaches and clothes must be made. I have neglected the sewing too long.

'There is, as I told you, no chance of my returning to work, but in my secret times I have started to make framed pictures out of dried flowers and grasses woven into tapestry, with embroidered lines of some of our most special poems underneath. I think you would be very charmed by my selection. I am sending you the first one finished, which I hope you can find a place for. Please comment truthfully. Making the pictures is intensely difficult and time-consuming, but utterly satisfying.

'Wait for it dear friend ... they can't entirely keep the Auld NAG down ... *I am now thinking of marketing my pictures!* What do you think of that idea?'

Last Letter: Nancy-Amelia still at home

'The good news first: I sold my first framed grass and flower picture for £20. There is no other good news, except that the health of all here is passable.

'However, I have a new strategy for getting through my wifely day. After I get up at six a.m. to see the Old Man off with my praise and duty kiss, I draw my pudgy self up to my full height in front of the long mirror, and speak the delicate word "bollocks" out loud. Then the girl in the mirror and I grin conspiratorially at one another. Well, for one brought up as the young woman I was, it is a very powerful thing to do. It is surprising how good it makes one feel. I do not understand why they don't teach you this in educational establishments.

'After the "bollocks" has come out real loud, it is a nip down to the kitchen to fill up a new hot water bottle. Then up to bed again for a sneaky read and some positively wicked thinking, before the real getting up and the day's chores, and the waiting for the men to come home, begins.

'I can firmly recommend the bollocks and the hot bottle treatment to any woman who feels used by those about her.'

Nancy-Amelia Garnett has tried to create a harmonious home, though she knows it is at the expense of herself. She lives a false life, a 'pretend' existence; for her husband's sake, she pretends to be someone other than she is and that he is someone other than he is – the boss, the man who knows everything, the one who is the rightful centre of her existence. We do not know if he is happy: we know that for much of the time she is not.

There is no doubt that all human relationships require concessions; the doubt is whether the concessions should all be one way. Are men – all men, some men, a few men? – are men only content, pleased, at ease, when they feel superior to women, and does this mean that women must *diminish* themselves in order to *enlarge* the men, as Cicely Hamilton maintained in 1909? Is this the fundamental inequality between the sexes which will defy all forms of legislation and which will continue to 'keep up appearances' so that men look big while women look small? Because the women feel that there is no alternative?

For Doris and Nancy-Amelia it seemed that there was no way of reconciling self-realisation with family harmony. Yet Florence, who was of the same generation, had achieved much of her self-realisation in the creation of family harmony. It could be that all this means is that human beings are different, that what works for some doesn't work for others. That whether or not a woman has to *give up* her self or whether she can *find* herself in the maintenance of a harmonious home depends after all on the individual woman – or man.

But to see the reflection of men and the way women handle it simply as the 'personal problem' of certain individuals, is to deny all the influences, pressures and structures which help to push women towards the management of men and to develop in men the expectation that such consideration is their due. Where did Doris, Nancy-Amelia and Florence get the idea that they were supposed to manage men? Moreover, where did the men get the idea that they were entitled to favoured treatment? Why is it that the women see the creation of harmonious relationships as *their* responsibility, while men do not?

While it is obvious that individuals make personal adjustments to the requirements of social belief and social order, this does not negate the existence of those beliefs and that order which place men in a primary position and which seek women's acquiescence. Some women find that acquiescence more painful and more penalising than do others.

This is the interpretation that we have been led to in our interviews with women. That *all* women reflect men, but that some find it worth the effort, and others do not; that some find it no great demand, and others find it draining and deadening.

Given the accounts of Florence, Doris and Nancy-Amelia (and Florence's explanations of the younger generation of less appreciative husbands), we have been puzzled by the contradictory messages of the media which currently suggest that there is now a 'new man' emerging, who takes a much greater share of the responsibility for home and children, and who makes many fewer 'emotional' demands on women than his father and grandfather before him.

There have been scores of articles, across the spectrum of women's magazines, which suggest that greater equality between the sexes is emerging as women move into paid work and as men move into the sphere of homemaking activities. We are led to believe that many sex-role distinctions are collapsing and that far from dismissing the traditional female values of nurturance, there are now many men who seek to acquire them. There is a new breed of men who are more concerned with giving rather than taking emotional support. Hence their greater involvement with children. Like Florence, many of the women we have interviewed think that women today continue to provide the emotional resources in the home and that their contribution is not appreciated. And like Florence many women believe that the situation is worse for women now than it has been in the past.

Some hold the women's movement directly responsible for the undesirable developments. They point to the fierce feminist denunciations of women's oppression within the family and declare that it was this which was responsible for undermining and breaking up the family unit. They quote the feminist demand for women's financial independence as the reason for women's increased entry to paid work. They quote the quest for sex equality as the reason for the devaluation of women's traditional nurturing role. And for the women who think it's all feminism's fault, a return to the good old days – when women did not work outside the home and were appreciated for what they did within it – would be quite an improvement.

If only it were so simple.

What gets left out of this particular line of reasoning is that no matter how far back we go, we are never going to reach the stage where women were only responsible for the family. Working-class women have almost always had paid work. Deserted wives, too, widows with dependent children and wives with profligate husbands have usually worked. They have worked for the very same reason that many women today are in paid work: because they *have* to. And it would not be an improvement for those women who *must* work if they are prevented from doing so.

The image of the nuclear family with working husband, 'economically inactive' wife and two children *is* an image. Few people realise how far removed from reality this image actually is. In an attempt to set the record straight, the Equal Opportunities Commission regularly publishes a bulletin *The Fact About Women is* . . . The 1983 edition contains the following entry:

Only five percent of all households are made up of working husband, economically inactive wife and two children.

The nuclear family is rare; it is absurd to think that society is composed of nuclear families and it is even more absurd to base policies on this assumption. If it ever *were* possible to return to the idealistic nuclear family existence, it is no longer. And to suggest, as some people do (particularly when they want a solution to male unemployment), that the world would be a better place if women were evicted from the workplace and forced to go home, would not only be grossly unrealistic, it would also be another example of the wholesale denial of women's needs.

Even though it might be possible to remove women from the workforce (after all, it has been done before*), the existence of the nuclear family does not depend solely on the wife being at home. It also depends on the husband providing her and the children with financial support. There are no guarantees on this issue: there were defaulters in the past; there are defaulters today. If Barbara Ehrenreich (1983) is right, there are few, if any, means of 'persuading' men to assume a breadwinning responsibility.

When women like Florence see that wives are now being asked to do more – the 'old' work of emotional support and the 'new' work of financial support – they, reasonably, suggest that something must give under the strain. Perhaps the cost can be measured in the breakdown of emotional support within the family. But if this is so, it is most certainly not the *fault* of the working wives who are being required to do more than is humanly possible.

Florence understood this. She did not blame her daughters; she blamed their husbands. She was more articulate than most women on the security which a happy family could provide (and which she saw as necessary and a wonderful contribution for women to make); in the interest of harmony and happiness she advocated a novel solution. The husband was just too much. If his demands were too great and his contribution to family harmony too little, both the problem and the solution were obvious. After a

---

* This was done directly in Britain (and other countries) during the 1920s when a 'marriage bar' was introduced and women were required to resign their paid work on marriage. It was done indirectly after the Second World War when propaganda played a part in convincing women that their proper place was in the home.

divorce, her daughter was part of a stable emotional unit where harmony prevailed even though there were financial problems.

A few (not many) women shared Florence's view of the problem and the solution. Annie was one woman who was adamant that she had less work and more joy now that she was on her own with her children. She had less money too. But to her the financial disadvantages were as nothing in comparison to the emotional – and work – advantages of single-parent family existence. She was convinced that both she and her children were in a much better emotional state without a 'head' of the family. For her, harmony in the home had been achieved by leaving him.

But is this the only answer? Should Doris and Nancy-Amelia have been counselled to leave their husbands? Would they have been happier if they had? Surely it is not the case that women can only find self-realisation apart from men – because men cannot change, cannot accept the equal rights of women?

This is a serious issue. If we put together Hilda Scott's statistics on the increase in the number of families headed by women, with Barbara Ehrenreich's thesis that an increasing number of men are no longer prepared to provide for their dependents, then what does this suggest about the future? That we are heading for a society where 'families' contain women and children, and where men are a nomadic population?

The majority of women we interviewed still, and for all sorts of reasons, see the family as necessarily containing a man, and a man who is seen to be the head of the house. And of these women, it is fair to say that about one third of them, far from seeing the women's liberation movement and sexual equality as desirable, actually see 'women's lib' as responsible for most of the contemporary problems of the devaluations of women's traditional role, and the defaults of men.

Betty Friedan (1982) agrees that mistakes have been made and that now there must be an all-out effort to bring men back into the family fold to share 'women's work'. Judith Stacey (1983) argues that the women's movement provided a critique of the family without 'providing models or visions of alternatives to conventional family structures' (p.575). According to Stacey, although the family structure may be limited and limiting, many want to try to make it work because nurture, support and intimacy are precious in an increasingly alienating and impersonal world. This might not be the precise way many women would put it, but they certainly shared Judith Stacey's sentiment and were absolutely determined to make the family work – emotionally.

'I want to be there for *all* of them,' Elena said of her husband and two children. 'I want to "mother" all of them. I *want* to do that. I chose my husband. I chose to have my children. I just have to *make* the time to meet all their needs. That's what being there is all about. If it takes every hour of the day to do it – well. So, it's a big job.'

Only three women (Elena was among them) did not distinguish the emotional management of their husbands from that of their children. They did not see any conflict between caring for their husbands and caring for their children but spoke in terms of emotional support of the *family* in the context of a commitment to moral principle.

Most women, however, freely admitted that they felt there was a constant tug of war going on between husband and children and that the only resolution lay in putting the husband first.

'I got a dreadful shock when Sharon was born,' Vida said, relating a not atypical story. 'I was just so pleased with her. It took me days to work out why my husband wasn't pleased. Why he was so upset. He was jealous. I know now. I was giving all my attention to the baby – and what about him? So I had to start making an extra effort with him. The doctor said it was normal. Happens to everybody. Said just make him feel he's still the most important person in your life. That's what I do now. Anyway, it wouldn't be much good for the baby to have a bad-tempered father.'

Again and again we were given accounts which matched those of Doris, Nancy-Amelia, and Florence's daughters, and which suggested that this is no 'personal problem'. Accounts of husbands who sulked and caused havoc if they felt that they were not getting enough attention. And, again and again, we found women who were not catering to the demands of their husbands for the simple sake of keeping them happy, but who had the explicit aim of providing a more harmonious home for the children. 'If he's in a bad mood, we *all* get it,' Celia said quite straightforwardly. 'So, he comes first. I get him sorted out then we can all have some peace. It means I have to send the kids out a lot. I've got a stack of things I send them off to do. When they get back I've usually got him fixed up. Doesn't take much. A bit of playing up to him and it's all O.K. I think I'd say we were a pretty happy family. As things go.'

One extraordinary feature which emerged in our discussions with women was the extent to which so many men are kept in ignorance about the realities of their own families: 'My husband lives in fantasy land,' Natalie said dryly. 'And I supply most of the fantasy. That he's important. That he's made his mark in the world. That his kids are a credit to him. Our daughter has been living with a man for almost five years, but he doesn't know that. And it would be the end of one big happy family if he ever found out. That's why I keep him in the dark about so many things.'

Nora's case was much the same. 'My son is gay,' she said. 'If my husband knew, he'd never want to see him again. It would destroy him. Well, I don't want to see my husband in a state and I don't want to lose touch with my son. So I make sure my husband doesn't find out.'

It was not always a grave or momentous issue which induced women to mislead their husbands. As Natalie said, 'Look, if I thought it would put him out to discover just how much a loaf of bread costs, I'd tell him it was half the real price.' She quite cheerfully remarked that if she ever left him he would be in for 'one helluva shock'.

There *were* women like Florence who had found satisfaction in managing men and who felt that it was their contribution to a good life. But they were women who believed they had a good life, and the sobering realisation is that so many women do not think their lives *are* good. For Florence, who was adamant that her husband was kind – and *reasonable* – and who firmly believed that she had the best that life could offer, the effort that she had made to manage her man was more than worthwhile.

Such satisfaction, we must emphasise, is the exception and not the rule. And not because women do not want to create harmony in the home but because, for personal, financial, 'structural' reasons, the attainment of such an 'ideal' is beyond them.

No woman said she did not want to create a harmonious family context. But *all* the women who said that this was one of their aims in life took it for granted that the lynch-pin was to make the man feel he was at the centre of concern. Some thought that this took too much time away from their contribution to their children's welfare; some saw it as a contribution they made to their children's welfare; some felt that it took too much from their own growth and development; some saw it as their own growth and development. Whatever the advantages or disadvantages of putting the man first, there was no 'happy family' where the woman did not insist that the fundamental requirement for a happy family was to put the man first. For some women this was a bigger burden than it was for others but for all women who wanted to create an emotional resource for their family in a hostile world, managing the emotional needs of men was a priority.

8

SANCTIONS

Despite the picture given so far in this book, *not* all women reflect men.

Some women don't.

However, the realistic and harsh evidence from most of our interviewees is that very few of the women who do not buy into the male adulation system, who stand up for themselves or who speak up for other women, survive unscathed. The bulk of our material reveals that women who refuse to please or placate men rarely get away with it.

Sanctions of some kind will be imposed.

Of course there are women who try not to reflect men, at least in their own homes, and many of these are committed feminists. If they live with men these feminists spend much of their domestic lives insisting on their right to independent thought; to an autonomous lifestyle, to not doing more for their male lovers or husbands than the men do for them, and never building up the men's egos unless it is totally reciprocated.

The feminists who found themselves in this situation admitted that what they suffered was constant emotional exhaustion. Trudy, who has been a warden in an old people's home for thirty-six years told us: 'I won't be ground down any more by the men I live with. If I had to do more for Victor than he was prepared to do for me, it would be irreconcilable with my politics. So I don't. But it *is* wearying. It is a constant battle against sexism. Some days truly it becomes easier to reflect.'

Other women we talked to avoided the issue of reflecting men on the domestic front by choosing to live alone or with other feminists, either as unmarried or unattached heterosexuals, or as lesbians who did not relate sexually to men and for the most part did not live with them.

When they lived as closet (or even open) lesbian mothers, these women encountered great pressure to reflect their children's fathers.

Rachel, a twenty-seven-year-old mother of two girls, who described herself as a quiet bisexual, said: 'I had long ago been separated from Jenny and Janet's dad. I had stopped feeling anything for him and frankly couldn't stand him near me. I certainly had no respect for him. Yet at Christmas I was still required to buy him an expensive present and ask him over for a Christmas dinner which I had to slave over while he watched. Throughout the whole – to me funereal – occasion I was required to make flattering remarks. I knew if I didn't play happy families when he wanted me to, he'd have the kids taken away.'

Sarah, aged thirty, who had one small boy, said, 'When my husband discovered I'd slept with a woman and I wanted to leave he refused to divorce me. For the last three years he has subtly forced me to look up to him as a "good father" and treated me as a "bad mother".'

None of these feminists escaped sanctions that were imposed on them at *work* when they refused to conform to the expected behaviour pattern.

If those who tried to tackle the issue of how to avoid male reflection in the house were *not* sturdy and principled feminists like Trudy, they were often women like Nancy-Amelia Garnett (Chapter Seven) who would not have called themselves feminists but who battled courageously for what they termed 'an even-stevens relationship'. These women too had great expectations of themselves and their partners.

Few of them steered a non-reflective course without encountering threats, abuse or hostility. We discovered that the greater their expectations, the less they reflected men, the higher the casualty rate.

Many women told us that they seemed to be succeeding until one day, in their men's view, they went 'too far'.

'I overstepped the limits.' (Janet, aged twenty-six)
'Went beyond the bounds.' (Erin, aged forty)
'Stepped out of line at work.' (Susan, aged twenty-nine)
'Argued with my superior.' (Lyn, aged thirty-three)

'Said something too provocative at home.' (Christine, aged nineteen)

'Forgot to smile.' (Gill, aged twenty-eight)

'Was too tired to face or fake an orgasm.' (Jenny, aged thirty-five)

'Demanded he paid attention to *me*.' (Meriel, aged thirty)

It was then that these women paid the price. It is a dreadful list to put forward.

Janet was slapped across the face by her boyfriend. Erin was hit about and pushed down a flight of stairs by her husband. Susan was consistently put down by her male boss in front of her colleagues and made to look stupid. Lyn was sent minutes for meetings *after* they had occurred, so that she could not have her say. Christine became the butt of her husband's contemptuous remarks in front of their friends. Gill was hit across the face and then pushed out of a moving car by her husband, broke her arm and wrist and badly injured her shoulder, back, and one leg. Jenny had tufts of her hair torn out and then was raped by her husband. Meriel's boyfriend walked out on her and their young baby.

The price, as you see, varies.

In the *workplace*, sanctions for non-conforming women range from patronisation, exclusion from major decision-making processes, failure to achieve promotion, to sexual harassment.

In the workplace, sexual demands between male boss and female employee are particularly coercive because women's economic livelihood is clearly at stake.

'I had a very responsible job in the civil service. I tried to retain my autonomy and not defer obsequiously to my boss. I felt there should be no need. However, it was important that I remained discreet about my personal life, as I lived with another woman who was also in the service. She was a temporary secretary. My boss kept asking me out to dinner and drinks. I think he suspected that I was a lesbian. He started making passes at me in office hours. Finally, I gave in. If I wanted to keep my job, I didn't have any choice. After three months I was so strained and tense I resigned. He refused to give me a reference' (Toni, aged thirty-six).

We discovered from our interviewees that, though all women must reflect in the workplace more than anywhere else, men's power to enforce their sex-role stereotyping on unwilling women was particularly crucial to the employment of feminist or lesbian women.

Until 1976, no one had a name for the disturbing condition that we now know as sexual harassment. Surveys since that date show that both in the USA and Great Britain this social phenomenon, which we believe is used frequently as a sanction for women's non-reflective behaviour at work, has highly significant consequences for *all* women's employment situations, and prospects.

Surveys since 1981 in both the USA and the UK suggest a range of figures from one in five, to four in five women who have reported experiencing various forms of sexual harassment. Probably the most useful survey to date comes from the USA where in 1981 the US Merit Systems Protection Board questioned 23,000 federal employees and found the incidence of sexual harassment experienced by respondents within the two years prior to the survey to be as high as 42%.*

In Britain the figures are comparable to those in the USA. In 1981, TV Eye, in conjunction with NALGO, conducted a survey of Liverpool City Treasurers Department. Of the women who responded, 36% reported experiences of sexual harassment at work.

A year later, in 1982, the Alfred Marks Bureau made inquiries of their 799 managers and employees in their branches throughout the UK: 66% of the employees and 86% of the management reported that they were aware of various forms of sexual harassment in their offices, and 51% of females admitted experiencing some form of sexual harassment in their working situations.

It is obvious even from these figures alone that sexual harassment is a widespread, typical, even an endemic feature of women's work.

What we discovered from our research is that it not only affects paid work. The following example, from a woman student at an Oxford college, was one of many incidents reported to us by young women 'working' at their studies in educational establishments.

'I know my work has gone downhill. I stopped going to supervisions. Every time I went to Dr Winter, he would stare at my breasts as I read out my essay. Whenever I ventured to disagree with him, he would touch them "accidentally". He kept

---

* For analysis of this survey, see Susan E. Martin (1981).

asking me out for drinks. I didn't want to go but I knew he had power over my grades' (Janine, aged twenty).

In the *home*, sanctions may veer from threats about custody control (these may escalate if the 'erring' wife has evidenced any extreme non-reflective signs such as bisexuality), to the terrifying practice, more widespread than is generally acknowledged, of sexually abusing young daughters of 'misbehaving' wives.

From some of the women we talked to, it appears that incest is a frequently but silently used weapon in the struggle for control in the ordinary household. In many homes we entered, father, mother and daughter were all aware of either the disquieting threat of child sexual assault, or the grim reality of its presence . . . but none of them even mentioned it.

Betty had just come through a gruelling divorce case when we met her. She looked older than her thirty-six years. After many years of marriage and being forbidden to work, or go out anywhere with the few friends she possessed, she had 'broken out' and got a job in an old people's home.

'That was when the real trouble started,' she told us. 'He'd always kept me back, made me stay in, hidden me from his friends and workmates. I was just there to serve him and the two girls. One was ours, the seven-year-old, the other was a lovely kid I fostered. She was eleven years old. Sometimes I thought he paid the girls more attention than me, ruffled them up, ran his hands over them a lot, you know the sort of thing, but I didn't think much of it. Until things got really bad between us. He said my work with the old people was making me look even uglier. He resented the hours I spent at the home talking to the old ladies. He said my tiredness interfered with our sex life. Well, that was a laugh, we'd never had a real sex life. Just him thrusting it in my mouth and holding me down. What was worse he'd never let me go to a cinema or a pub or anywhere apart from Tesco's. One day, I'd had enough. It was late-night shopping for the elderly in the city. I promised I'd take my old ladies. I told him I was going with them, and that we planned to have a meal afterwards. He was like thunder. Roughed me up worse than usual and said if I went he'd teach me a lesson.'

Betty went to town with her old ladies. When she returned he had put a lock on her bedroom door. Every night thereafter he made her go to bed early and he locked her in, while he stayed downstairs with the two little girls. ' "I'll get them off to bed,

OK?" he would say,' she told us, crying at the still recent memories. 'There were strange stifled noises from the telly-room and I heard my own daughter cry out. But he used to take her up to bed and stay downstairs with our foster child. Then there would be more noises and he'd turn the telly up real loud. Finally, he'd go into the next room to ours and stay with the girls for a long time. I could hear them crying but I was powerless to go into them. It took me three years before I had enough guts to admit to myself that he was, you know, doing it to them. Oh god, I wish I'd never stood up to him. It's made us all feel so cheap and dirty.'

We wish that Betty's story was the only one. Unfortunately both research done for this book, and research done for other recent studies in the USA and Great Britain, shows that it is not.

Rebecca and Russell Dobash (1979) show that children are the second most common victim of family assault (wives are the first). And a UK study of the incidence of sexual abuse by Beezley Mrazek, P., Lynch, M. and Bentovim, A. (1981) found that 85% of victims were girls. They also discovered (a fact that tallies with Betty's story) that sexual abuse begins very early. 13% of the victims were under six years. 27% were between six years and ten years. 60% were over eleven years.

Elizabeth Stanho (1985) points out that the pattern of incest is one in which in 90% to 97% of cases the offender is male, and that in 87% of cases the person assaulted is female. Which helps to account for the recent additional category in sexual abuse; that of 'father–daughter rape' (see Elizabeth Ward, 1984). The 1976 Home Office report claims that 72% of convicted incest offenders are fathers.

Judith Lewis Herman, author of *Father–Daughter Incest* (1981), carefully examined five American surveys about incest. She discovered that one-fifth to one-third of all women reported they had had some sort of childhood sexual encounter with an adult male; that between 4% and 12% of all women reported a sexual experience with a relative, and one woman in every hundred reported sexual experiences with father or stepfather. The offender, though not necessarily the father, is usually a trusted adult, such as grandfather, stepfather, uncle or close male friend of the family (Sandra Butler, 1979; Beezley Mrazek *et al*, 1981).

Few respondents reported these incidents. None of the women we interviewed for this book, many of whom reluctantly revealed bitter and shaming stories like Betty's, had ever told anyone either of the father-daughter rapes in their own early lives or the, in their view more harrowing, husband-daughter rapes, which many of them felt were a result of their own mismanagement, a product of their own failure.

David Finkelhor (1979) emphasises that the vast majority of children *never* tell anybody about incestuous assault, and he estimates that 75% to 90% of incidents are never discovered.

We would go even further and suggest that because many wives and girlfriends believe they have brought this sexual terror into their daughters' lives by their own non-appeasing behaviour, they are too ashamed for the most part to report incidents which they are well aware are happening to their own children.

The threat of violence is as significant a factor as actual violence in ensuring that women will toe the line. We discovered during the course of our interviews, that women know that potential violence can be used as a reminder to women that they must 'make allowances' for men; that they are not in a position to obstruct or thwart, but must endure, no matter how painful or shaming they find it. This is not just the case with incest. There is a whole range of threats which serve as reminders that women cannot act but are acted upon; from the apparently innocuous wolf-whistle and verbal abuse in the streets, right through to assault. Women have grown up learning to read these cues, learning the danger signs, learning when to look down, look away, 'turn a blind eye'. Most accept that this is part of male-female relations.

Many women we talked to said casually; 'Of course he hit me about, but I couldn't do anything, I was married to him.'

We believe all these actions are contrivances both designed to keep women in line, and more specifically to punish those who step out of line, who refuse to mirror men adequately. In a society which is officially no longer authoritarian, violent measures are useful to boyfriends and husbands as a way of reinstating patriarchal authority.

Emily, aged thirty-eight, the wife of a steel worker, told a grim tale that was almost beyond bearing. 'In the beginning he only hit me when I didn't listen to him properly or couldn't keep the kids quiet when he wanted to have his say. After the first five years it was the way I dressed, or the things I said, or speaking to my friends on the phone, or going down Mum's, or if I didn't agree at once.

'By that time he'd fractured me cheekbone twice, and me legs and back were so badly done in I had to have a stick. But by then he was lashing out even when I didn't complain at all.

'I knew I couldn't leave. I was his wife. I knew I had to try and be more what he wanted, if I was to avoid getting the worst of it. What else could I do, after all I was wed wasn't I? I kept myself going, thinking if I could please him more tomorrow it might stop. But it never did.'

Violence such as Emily (and others) described to us, and more importantly, the *threat* of such violence, has been central to women's oppression. Historically, it has been an essential part of establishing and maintaining the kind of family common in the Victorian era.

It came about because in pre-capitalist and early capitalist societies in Western Europe, battering was maintained by stringent moral and legal codes. Rebecca and Russell Dobash (1979) point out that Christianity provided ideological reasons for these patriarchal marriages, and that then those social relations were codified into law by the male-run state. That allowed the family to be overtly established as the domain of the husband by marriage laws which forced wives to conform to their husbands' will and wishes, and which punished husbands and wives unequally.

'To be a wife meant becoming the property of a husband, taking a secondary position in a marital hierarchy of power and worth, being legally and morally bound to obey the will and wishes of one's husband, and thus quite logically, subject to his control even to the point of physical chastisement or murder' (Dobash and Dobash, p.33).

In the seventeenth, eighteenth and nineteenth centuries in England any husband could legally beat his wife in the home, provided he used a stick no thicker than a man's thumb.

In America, although the husband's rights were not present in legal statutes, their right to chastise their wives was upheld in 1824 by the Supreme Court of Mississippi. The Court ruled that a husband should be allowed to chastise without being subject to vexatious prosecution which would supposedly shame all parties (ibid., p.62).

It was not until 1829 in England that the husband's absolute power of chastisement was abolished, and not until 1871 in the USA was wife battering for the first time declared illegal in two States, Massachusetts and Alabama (ibid., p.63).

Despite the fact that nineteenth-century feminists struggled against their very definition as the property of their husbands, violence against women generally and wives in particular continued. Even today, police are reluctant to intrude on what they term a 'domestic matter'.

In the twentieth century, husbands are not legally allowed their bullying status, but many husbands of women we interviewed seem to overlook that fact. Today, although they do not legally own wives, a great many of the husbands involved with the women in this book continue to behave as if they did. If recent figures for battering are any indication, men today have just as big an investment in retaining power and control in the marital home as they did yesterday.

How widespread is this phenomenon? In Britain in 1975 the Select Committee on Violence in Marriage recommended that there should be one family place (which is a place for a woman and her children) in a battered aid refuge per every 10,000 of the population in order to meet the needs of women abused in the home. In 1977 the British divorce statistics indicated violence in 50% of the 685,000 marriages dissolved.

Estimates to establish the incidence of violent assault in the USA suggest that in a population of approximately 200 million, 1.8 million women living in heterosexual couples are beaten each year. Women who are separated or divorced are also estimated to be at risk from assault, which would give a total of two to six million women abused each year by their male partners. Estimates are that only 10% of this violence involves an isolated event, the other 90% involves systematic beatings, often with escalating violence during the course of the marriage.

At the same time, physical abuse was cited as grounds for separation and divorce in one-third to one-half of US petitions (Jalna Hanmer, 1983).

Once more, as with incest and sexual harassment, the numbers in published statistics are but a tiny proportion of the violent crime that has actually taken place. We know from the women we have spent hours speaking to that silence about assault is the norm not the exception. Many women were reluctant even to talk to us, and would not have dreamt of reporting assaults officially.

Backing up what we now know to be the case, come findings from the Dobashes who discovered that less than 3% of all physical attacks by husbands and other known men on women were reported to the police; and findings by Jalna Hanmer and Sheila Saunders (1983) in their Leeds study, which found that only 11% of incidents were reported to the police.

We interviewed Wendy, who, after ten years of being both raped and battered, finally and in terrible fear of her life decided to go to her doctor rather than the police. She told us: 'Fred was my man so I couldn't tell no one official could I? Also, Fred told me I wasn't giving him satisfaction no more in bed. Well, I couldn't, could I? Not with me stitches torn out? But I couldn't report it, not when it was my fault, could I?'

Even if Wendy had reported Fred's behaviour she might not have found a very sympathetic ear. For, despite the fact that the three characteristics of violent behaviour processed by police and courts are that physical and sexual assault is overwhelmingly carried out by men, that inside the family men are more likely to assault women than other men, and that a quarter of all recorded violent crime is wife assault, the police force does little to help wives like Wendy.

We feel that not enough studies look at the relationship between victim and offender. Certainly in assessing violence as a sanction for non-reflective behaviour, that relationship is crucial.

The Dobash study does consider this relationship. It found that of 3,020 accounts of inter-personal violence, wife assault was the second most common crime (being 25% of crimes noted by the police), and violence from husbands constituted 72% of all violence against women. The Dobashes pointed out that, given the unwillingness of the police to charge cohabitees and husbands, it would probably be accurate to say that it is the most common form of violent crime. They found that women were much more likely to be assaulted by men who were known to them than by strangers and this was borne out in our research.

The experiences of British agencies like Rape Crisis Centres and Women's Aid would confirm this. They established that, firstly, the more intimate the relationship, the more likely women are to be assaulted, and secondly, the more intimate the relationship the more likely women are to be subjected to repeated attacks.

Wendy, who had been married ten years and had five small

children, the last three by caesarean, makes the point better than we can. 'After them operations, I'd been really badly ill but Fred would never leave me alone. In bed I mean. Not even when I was ruptured with stitches and my whole body felt torn. He just kept jumping on me demanding it. When I told him how much it hurt and how me mum had said it's best to rest up, he got real mad. I brought his heat on worse and he ripped my clothing off and held me down while he did it. Each time, he did it more horrible. So I cried out and then he said I wasn't treating him right and he wouldn't let me stop him. He knotted my hands to the bedpost and had his way. I've never known him so angry. I was a terrible mess, the stitches came out, blood everywhere, the pain was awful. He was disgusted with me. By the time of the fifth baby, I could hardly walk but Fred wanted it even more often, said I was rebelling and he'd teach me not to rebel. He threatened to kill me if I didn't give in to him and I couldn't tell my mum that, could I? I had one friend I told and she said it was rape but it couldn't be because I was married. But he read a letter from her to me, and he cut my wrist while he had me, to teach me not to write notes. I couldn't go to the police like I told you, so I went to our doctor him being an expert. Of course, I put Fred in as good a light as possible. I just said the pains were bad and I was frightened of being killed if I didn't satisfy Fred. The doctor looked really cold at me and said "Then you'd better satisfy him, my dear".'

Wendy's experience showed that battering was reinforced by marital rape as a weapon to bring her to heel. But no matter how far terror-struck women may try to placate men, attacks may continue.

Petra, wife of the civilised, cultured John, said that when she was breast feeding at four-hourly intervals, too tired to make love, John threw her on the sofa in front of the children and told them, 'Your mother's a whore, she sleeps with everyone in the neighbourhood except your father.' Then he held her down in a chair and bashed her head against the wall over and over again until she said she wanted sex.

'Then he dragged me on to the bed, jumping viciously on me, wham bang, you could almost call it rape. From that point on, sex always made me cry. He thought the tears were a measure of my ecstasy, but it was my total humiliation. Not once in ten years did I do it because I wanted to. At the end of my married life, I could not walk past that bed without bursting into tears.'

Petra's and Wendy's stories of the intricate connection between battering and rape, and the likelihood of repeated attacks within intimate relationships, are borne out by two recent studies by Diana E. H. Russell and Irene Hanson Frieze.

Diana Russell's study, 1975, revealed that 21% of women who had ever been married reported physical violence by a husband at some time in their married lives; and also showed that 10% of the respondents reported being raped as well as battered.

Irene Frieze's (1983) research amongst battered women in the USA showed that one in every three women she interviewed had been battered; but in addition, of the battered women, one-third had also been raped, and two-thirds felt they had been pressured into having sex with their husbands.

In both studies, as in our interviews, few of the attacks were isolated incidents. The women they talked to, like the women we talked to, found it hard to equate their husband's 'normal' if high-handed sexual behaviour with a word like 'rape'.

'She said it was rape but it couldn't be because I was married,' Wendy said.

'Jumping viciously on me, wham bang, you could almost call it rape,' Petra said.

This is because there are widely held myths that rape only occurs with strangers in dark alleys or across deserted commons or from sex perverts; that rapes are premeditated acts of sex; and that women both provoke and enjoy rape. The facts, of course, are in direct contrast.

Most rapes are committed by normal men. Most rapes are by known men. Many rapes are planned in advance. Rapists often use weapons. Rape victims suffer both short- and long-term traumas far removed from pleasure. Women do not invite rape. Rapes, in general, are acts of power not acts of sex, as was very obvious from the behaviour of Petra's civilised husband and Wendy's 'teacher' husband.

Fred said that Wendy was rebelling and that what he did to her was to teach her not to rebel. What he did to her was to beat her up and rape her. Wendy, far from rebelling, became seriously ill, mentally and physically, with the strain of trying to reflect and placate him, in order to ward off even worse violence. But as Petra said to us, 'You can never reflect them enough to stop their anger.'

It is, of course, difficult to establish the incidence of rape, or even to document the grim reality of rape in ordinary womens' lives, largely because of the gap between how rape is experienced by women and how rape is counted as a criminal offence by police. Reported rapes only constitute a minute proportion of serious crimes. Rape crisis centres which have been working on both sides of the Atlantic to help rape and incest victims since 1970 have done research to suggest that *most* rapes are not reported, and they indicate that as many as 75% of rapes never reach the attention of the police at all. Since our evidence showed that many instances of rape were used in marriage and cohabitation as a punishment for inappropriate behaviour, this figure did not surprise us.

Of course, the price for non-conformity is not always as high as rape. For some women the sanctions attached to non-reflective behaviour are bearable, the damage slight. But even these lighter penalties are not necessarily more dealable with.

Several women told us that when they either forgot or decided not to heed Marabel Morgan's dictum that 'a Total Woman caters to her man's special quirks whether it be in salads, sex or sports' (p.60), the response of their men was not merely hostile, it was also unnerving and quite outside their control.

The sanctions these men imposed on women were violent or disgusting bodily actions which started with yawning or belching and degenerated to farting or the use of excrement, or exposing their genitals in public places.

Although these acts can only be described as 'mildly violent' they, like acts of extreme violence, are types of behaviour which women are unable to prevent and whose outcome they are unable to predict. This generally adds an extra dimension of fear to the victim's interpretation of that behaviour. We discovered from our interviewees that sometimes retaliation by men which is largely verbal or visual can be just as threatening (sometimes more so) to the woman than a blow in the face.

Meriel's boyfriend walked out on her and their baby after she demanded he pay her some attention. He returned one evening but did not enter the house or in any way verbally communicate with her. He stood outside the kitchen window where she was washing up and urinated up at the pane of glass.

'He could see me,' she told us. 'He didn't speak. When he had finished peeing he spat several times in my direction. Then slowly he began to masturbate; still with his penis up towards my window. I stood frozen. Terrified. I could not think of anything except what harm he might be planning me and the baby. When he'd done it, he spat again, and without a word walked silently away. I was shaking and burst into tears.'

Janet, a twenty-four-year-old worker in a tool-making factory, was another recipient of unnerving body actions. She told us that her husband Bill, a factory worker, gets in from work earlier than she does, but always expects her to get his tea, conceal her tiredness and 'listen, really sharp like, while he talks about his new promotion'.

Janet has to agree with him over everything he has said that day to the boss 'and tell him what a right clever one he is'. She says that as long as she keeps up this 'flattering natter, he's all awake and interested, and will even occasionally lay table for me. But if I show I'm fed up or tired, or try and talk about *my* day, he starts these great big yawns up in my face.'

Janet said that if she continues to discuss what her mates said on the line, he staggers over to the tea-table with a 'right surly look' and as soon she puts his tea down he gets this 'huge bout of indigestion, keeps belching and ignoring me. If I complain he yawns between belches and says he's worried his indigestion might make him throw up.'

Usually Janet gives up any attempt to interest him in her day and returns to talking about *his* job. 'Then, would you believe it, the big belches slow down and all them nasty yawns disappear. The whole thing is unnerving.'

Both Nancy Henley (1977, p.82) and Erving Goffman (1963, pp.128 & 288) who look at body language and power, talk about a variety of 'gross' body behaviours, ranging from spitting to passing gas, which though not countenanced in 'polite company' are used in private to show disgust, contempt or hostility.

Erving Goffman says that some of these offensive acts 'imply arrogance, disdain, deep hostility, as when a middle-class person yawns directly before others in a slow and elaborate manner' (p.288). As Janet's husband Bill illustrated, this is *not* confined to the middle classes.

Because actions like yawns and belches can be passed off as accidental or uncontrollable they serve as devices which can punish women without being punishable in return. Nor are these unpleasant sanctions as rare as we had imagined.

Mona, our interviewee, was criticised by other women for not sufficiently reflecting her son Tobias; she also tried to make it a policy not to reflect Mick, the man she lives with. She is not able, however, to carry out this policy without severe repercussions.

'His anger is always displayed physically. Probably because he is no match for me verbally. He throws things or makes foul uses of his body. That's when I won't send him back the message "Oh what a wonder man you are". Possibly he feels less of a man because I won't do it. Certainly he's very withdrawn.' Mona told us about an occasion when Mick, who works in the oil trade, was invited to a conference at a large hotel and suggested she and the children went along "all dressed up".

She said: 'He saw me as his handbag. An accessory that he wanted to look frilly and wife-like. I wouldn't do it. I haven't any frilly clothes. I said I'd go in clean dungarees and a new smart shirt. But I refused to take off my peace badge. He got so angry, first he threw the ironing board at me, then the iron. They caught my stomach and I was sick.'

Instead of going to the conference Mona stayed at home and listened to Woman's Hour on the radio. She heard a poem read aloud by a man who had been collecting African folk poetry. She said, 'It was called "Ode to a beautiful woman". The first line ran "Young lady you are a mirror" and the last line ran "You are an eagle feather worn by a husband". The stuff in the middle wasn't much better. Well I was astonished! I wondered whether those poor old African women who refused to mirror their husbands or act as eagle feathers to adorn their men, were treated to the physical contempt Mick puts me through.'

This physical contempt was so degrading, Mona said, that when she tried to tell other women they refused to listen. Mick uses farting, excreting and trampling animal mess across their floors in order to silence her if she is being what he calls 'aggressive'.

'If I've refused to boost him up over a particular issue, he doesn't argue, but later will come into the house with lots of dog shit on his very big feet. In he rushes, in his very big shoes, pretending to be in too much of a hurry to remove them. He dashes upstairs for something "urgent" then races from room to room spreading foul dog-shit. I stand and scream at him to take off his filthy shoes and clean up his filthy mess. But he won't do either. Each time it happens he pretends it is an accident. Then he mutters that he has just got time for a snack lunch, and he sits on a chair downstairs, gulping his snack, whistling and singing, watching me scrubbing up the dog-shit he's left, with bucket after bucket of disinfected water.'

Mona said no matter how hard she tries to persuade him to clean it up, he ignores her, refuses to answer, just sits, whistles and sings. 'I have no choice but to clean up after him. No woman with two small kids will leave that around.'

After some hours of discussion she decided to tell us about things which she said other women have shunned her for revealing. 'They all want us to protect men. They don't want us to

"MY FAMILY WERE ALL POTTY-TRAINED AT AN EARLY AGE. ALL EXCEPT MY HUSBAND, OF COURSE."

reveal the violent side of men's behaviour. They would rather believe my behaviour is foul than believe it of Mick.'

What kinds of male behaviour could be so distressing to women they would rather conceal them?

'If I've angered Mick by refusing to let him act the superior man, he punishes me by going to the loo, where he shits, then refuses to flush it after him. What can I do? With small children and a constant stream of visitors I can't *not* flush it. He knows that sooner or later I'll be forced to do it. When reluctantly I go upstairs to do so, he passes behind me "accidentally", whistling and singing, watching triumphantly as I flush away his shit.'

Mona says that every time she asks him to perform his own menial tasks he refuses. 'Not in words but by his actions. He doesn't answer. Just walks away. Never discusses it. Never does what I ask. Pretends he doesn't know what I'm on about. Some days it makes me feel I'm going mad. At first, I thought it was an accident. Then I realised it occured more and more as I began to flatter him less and less. He can't make me be what he wants, a docile flattering wife, but he can punish and frighten me with body actions which I can't predict and can't control. I used to think he was just spiteful, now I wonder if there's a deeper meaning.'

If Erving Goffman's and Nancy Henley's theories about body language are accurate, then Mona could be right. In most of their verbal interaction she is obviously the more powerful and according to Nancy Henley what Mick is doing is using gross physical actions as a 'power of disruption' which she says can become, in certain situations, 'the ultimate power of the powerless' (p.83).

Juliet works as a waitress in a large hotel in St Ives in Cornwall. Like Mona and Rosie she sees herself as a feminist, with as she puts it 'a definite gift of the gab'. She told us she can out-talk everyone 'men included' and she said she was not in the market to build them up unless they merited it. Juliet too lives with a man who uses body language to get back at her when she has chosen not to reflect him. In her case it is less for her non-placatory attitude than to shut her up as soon as she becomes critical.

'If I feel Ed is in the wrong, I say so. He doesn't argue back. First he lashes out. Either fists me sharply in the stomach or kicks me hard in the rear end. He pretends it is "playful" but he's a huge man, 6'4", about thirteen stone, and sometimes the whack he gives me hurts for days. Once he's clobbered me, he quietly walks away. He won't allow me to express any criticism or anger towards him. After giving me a physical jolt he often disappears for days. That silences me!'

Juliet explained that Ed will return as suddenly and unexpectedly as he vanished. 'I'm often so relieved I rush to give him an affectionate hug. But he hasn't forgotten that I criticised him, and as I go up behind him to put my arms affectionately round him, he contrives to fart, almost in my face. How on earth he manages it I don't know. I've tried to reason with him, each time it happens he says it is an accident. But it only happens on occasions when I've refused to please him, then want to show my love for him.'

As Erving Goffman (1963) said, farts are not punishable like any other retort. Nor, it seems from the distressed way in which Meriel, Janet, Mona and Juliet told their stories, are these distasteful bodily retorts the kind of actions you can talk about to your friends.

Juliet said: 'I haven't told other women. I know they wouldn't accept it from me. They would turn it back on me. They'd feel it reflected some nastiness in me rather than in him. That makes me really upset. I keep trying to have a realistic loving relationship with Ed, trying to praise him if it is deserved, not if it isn't. I try and show I care for him but want an honest understanding between us. He doesn't want that. He wants flattery. So he retaliates.

'I can't tell my women friends what happens when I don't pamper him, because they don't want to listen. Perhaps they find it threatening to their own situations.'

Because we were interested to know how widespread is the use of excrement as a means of punishment – and because we were acutely aware of the taboo which makes it unlikely that women would volunteer such information, we did directly ask women, on occasion, whether men used this as a way of making women 'toe the line'. And we were amazed at the response.

Many women had made the link between excrement and power. Eight women said that when their husbands were *not* pleased they expressed their displeasure in most antisocial ways. 'If I have my women friends round, Dick manages to walk through the sitting room and fart. He certainly lets me know he doesn't like it. And it works. I am reluctant to ask them round if I know he will be in.'

'My husband's speciality is his underpants. Skid marks, I believe they are called. There is a high correlation between skid marks and his temper. When it's bad, so are they. I get the message. It's not pleasant having to soak dirty underpants.'

'It amuses my fellah to fart in bed. And to push my head under the bed clothes. And it is *not* random. It's always when he has some gripe against me.'

'My husband soils his pants. Well, that's the nice way of saying it, isn't it. He shits them. And if I carry on about it, he shits them more. He tells me that it happens because he's nervous. If I don't want it, I shouldn't make him nervous. And it makes him nervous if I bring up the topic. So it's taboo. He goes on shitting his pants and I go on silently washing them. And *it is disgusting*. You have to do them separately. You can't put *that* in with the rest of the wash. You can't take a load like that to the laundromat. You have to do them at home – on their own. And every week when I boil those dirty pants, I know I've been had.'

This is no exaggeration. These are the words of women who were all concerned about their anonymity, who all believed that to divulge this information reflected on *them* – who came from all walks of life and from relationships that in other senses they stated were 'satisfactory'. Yet to us, this seems a far cry from love, romance and happy families. Yet by remaining silent, all of these women helped to support the appearance of the happy family.

But we do understand why women are silent, why women are scared. We do understand why women learn to live warily, to stay on guard, to *protect* themselves from onslaught and assault. We do understand why women develop survival strategies. Reflecting men is a primary survival strategy for women who are in subordinate positions, who fear male violence and violation, and who can never be sure when it will next occur.

Nancy-Amelia Garnett spoke for many of the women we interviewed when she said: 'If you want a harmless life don't get too uppity. You can have two fingers going up like train signals at the tea-table and even in bed, as long as your old man doesn't spot them. But you cannot indulge in deliberate and cold rebellion against the slow crucifixion of marriage and management of menfolk without reaping a pack of trouble.

'If you do, you'll regret it. They will bleed hot and heartfelt tears from you and leave you *fearing something worse*.'

She hit upon a particular phrase that rang true for almost every woman we encountered. The phrase 'fearing something worse' had a traumatic meaning for many of them. In nearly every transcript we played, that phrase recurred regularly.

Let us listen to just two voices. The voice of Venetia, who was forced to behave like a slave to her hero Marcus and the voice of Abbey, whose famous photographer husband blacked her eyes then complained she did not smile.

'Like I told you, Marcus was a terrible one for backhanding me one in the teeth if I didn't smile or praise him enough. One day he was going so fast in the car I was too scared to smile, particularly as I'd just failed my driving test and was nervous. So he gave me this backhander and you have to take into account he used to weight-lift, so I literally spun round. No one could smile, not spinning like that, even with the best intentions which I always had. But he couldn't take the spinning into account, and I knew there would be something worse.

'I shall never forget washing out the white sheepskin car covers afterwards because they'd got all soaked in blood, so it must have been something worse than usual. My mother would have been horrified at the state of his car as she'd always brought us up clean and tidy. But anything was possible with Marcus in a mood. That's what was sad, me and Marcus together all those years, we had a lot of possibilities, which were all wasted, all those years going to waste.'

And Abbey: 'By the end I'd stopped flattering him so I was never safe from his violence. I was knocked about so it wasn't worth Terry's while taking photos of me any more. Too much touching up to do. He had new young models by then and didn't need me. He didn't hit me regularly at first or on the face too much, just hard enough, often enough, to keep me in line. It also kept me silent because I felt ashamed of what he was doing to me. I kept smiling at him whenever humanly possible for fear he'd do something worse to me. He said if I told anyone he'd do something much worse so, of course, I didn't tell a soul for six years. Today, at forty, I look back at those years with Terry and it just seems such a waste, a waste of so many possibilities.'

It is worth noting that Nancy-Amelia, Venetia, Abbey, Petra, Wendy and the many other women we talked to make in their own individual ways the same point that Phyllis Chesler and Emily Jane Goodman make in *Women, Money and Power* (1976) and that Andrea Dworkin makes in *Right Wing Women* – that 'women struggle, in the manner of Sisyphus, to avoid the "something worse" that can and will always happen to them if they transgress the rigid boundaries of appropriate female behaviour' (Dworkin, 1983 p.15).

From the material we have gathered it seems that the essential ingredient, in appropriate female behaviour, is the ability to reflect men at twice their mirror image.

It is not only women who fear something worse. Men fear something worse too. What is interesting is that the objects of female and male fears are not only different but opposite. Margaret Atwood, Canadian feminist and writer, summed up this significant difference in a book called *Second Words* (1983). She asked a *male* friend of hers: 'Why do *men* feel threatened by women?' He replied: 'They are afraid women will laugh at them. Undercut their world view.' Then Margaret Atwood asked some *female* students: 'Why do *women* feel threatened by men?' The women replied: 'They are afraid of being killed.'

This savage indictment sums up the difference as we see it between female and male perspectives, and encapsulates the relationship between reflecting men as a process, and fear of violence as an explanation.

The 'something worse' that men fear is that women will stop reflecting them: stop adopting male values; stop seeing the world from a male viewpoint. Women cannot both laugh at men and flatter them hugely.

The 'something worse' that women fear is that men will express their anger through violence. They are afraid that men who have the power to be violent may exercise it. Even unto death.

In a society where women are systematically defined as inferior and, within marital property rights, sexually used and abused as of right, it is logical that just as the female process of reflecting men which begins with faint praise should end with fake orgasm, so should male sanctions that begin with contempt or dismissal end with some things that are much worse.

What we noticed in talking to these woman was that their fears were all intermingled with deep regrets for years and chances that had been wasted. We noticed many women, anguished at being beaten up or deserted, saw their lives as wastelands of unfulfilled possibilities. Frances, whose husband, Harry, having battered her for fifteen years, suddenly left her and three teenagers for someone younger, told us, 'I can't believe it of him. You've no idea how kind he is really. The Harry who batters me, forces me to have sex, and has deserted us, isn't the real Harry. I mustn't have done enough for him. If I believed all this of him, I'd know my *whole life had been wasted.'*

We are tempted to say will the real Harry, the real Marcus, the real Terry please stand up. Stop battering and raping the real women in your lives, and stand up and be counted. Counted and then be discounted.

For women do waste whole lives. Long lives. Lives that could have been spent productively. They waste them reflecting men so that the home can be happy. They waste them reflecting men because they fear what men will do if they are not happy. They believe if only they'd mollified, placated, smoothed and soothed a little better, a little more, the something worse would not have taken place. All their lives they've adhered to the rules for male reflection. Smile sweetly. Fake furiously. Laugh at their lousy jokes. Rescue them from idiocy. No matter what you feel like, no matter if you don't feel anything. Notice him. Pleasure him. Propitiate him. Do it all visibly. Audibly. No matter what he does, or doesn't do in return. *That's the rub.*

What many women have not yet noticed is that when men who do not adore us, men who do not protect us, men who do not build us up, deal us the final blow, that *is* something worse: even then we negotiate, barter, creep and flatter, because we are enmeshed in this idea that reflection will save us. And it will not. That idea is erroneous.

It might seem that if fear of violence is used to ensure that women will please men, and punish those who don't then it *ought* to be the case that women who don't reflect get battered, beaten, scarred and submerged; while good, kind, subservient, nurturing women who *do* reflect remain unharmed, safe and happy. *It is not so.*

Women who are seen to be uppity get punished. Often with violence. Women who reflect men all their lives get punished. Often with violence. Women who are battered, and hastily return to reflecting, get battered again. Sometimes batterers like Harry leave. Research shows that men who batter can move from one abusive relationship to another. There is nothing it seems women can do to ward off male violence. Women are correct to fear something worse. It is likely to happen. Women become guilty. Try harder. The cycle of flattering – failure – battering – guilt –

flattering – failure – battering – guilt – begins again and again.

As no matter what women do, violence may ensue, we believe that women should stop encouraging and colluding with men and with potential male violence by reflecting them.

As Petra says you can never reflect enough to ward off their anger. So we might as well stop now.

9

ASSERTIVENESS TRAINING IS NOT ENOUGH

"WHAT YOU REALLY MEAN IS ......"

Eighteen months and sixty thousand words ago we sat in a London restaurant and watched two women, obviously at ease, contentedly eating and talking together. The women were approached by a strange man who regarded them as 'alone' and therefore presumed them to be both interruptible and welcoming of his unwarranted intrusion. To our dismay, he was received not with a whimper but with a smile.

That smile, that incident, and our shock, set us on the trail of this book.

A steady stream of subservient smiles later, we sat in a Cambridge concert hall and watched an incident during a Holly Near folk singing recital which was no less shocking (although by now much less surprising). It was from this episode that we began to draw some conclusions.

The hall was packed with a large, liberal throng of 'right-on' women and men. Feminists. Radicals. Brown rice sisters. Folk song enthusiasts. SDP followers. White anti-sexist men. Alternative bookshop owners and browsers. University and technical college students and staff. The kind of audience that regarded themselves and each other as well read, intelligent, witty, cultured, stylish and, above all, considerate and caring of each others' needs. Towards the end of the show, Holly Near launched into a song called 'Perfect Night'.* She sang this first verse in a straightforward manner:

> The woman is dressed in style tonight
> She's got a three-piece suit and a tie tonight.
> There's a polished glow on her face in spite of her look of
>   amusement.
> And she will dine with her true love
> Take in a bar or two
> And nothing short of a perfect night will do.

Everyone was quietly beating time or humming. The singer continued, somewhat archly:

> The gal is dressed for work tonight.
> She's got dusty jeans and some boots tonight.
> There's a lover's look on her face in spite of her farming
>   intentions.
> And she will plant with her true love
> Take a break in the bar, maybe two
> And nothing short of a perfect night will do.

A few quick-witted women in the auditorium began to grin. Holly grinned back at them. 'They're getting there!' she quipped. Then, twinkling at the crowd, she threw out the first clue that her

---

* 'Perfect Night' Words by Holly Near. Music by Jeff Langley 1983, Hereford Music. Used on Holly Near and Ronnie Gilbert record 'Lifeline'.

polished lady may not be dining with the expectable male lover, after all:

> The jack is dressed in wool tonight
> She's got a baseball glove, a cap tonight.
> There's a competitive look in her eyes in spite of her generous
>   heart.
> And she'll play ball with her true love
> Take in a home run or two
> And nothing short of a perfect night will do.

All the women in the audience began to nudge each other and started to laugh. Most of the men managed a small smile. Some frostily. Some nervously. Then Holly Near delivered the body blow:

> All the rules have been broken
> They're not talking about the weather
> A gentleman asks 'Are you ladies alone?'
> They smile and say 'No, we're together.'

The crowd burst into wild gales of laughter and thunderous applause. The most consistent comment around the hall was 'Outrageous, simply outrageous!' The women were frankly amazed and admiring. 'What a brilliant retort,' one woman said. 'I only wish I could be brave enough to use it.'

'If only I could be that pushy,' remarked another.

'I just can't imagine myself making that comeback,' confirmed a particularly hardheaded feminist wistfully.

Several of the women we spoke to said, 'I bet it makes the men change their minds and think again.'

Did it? Does it? This is what we heard three of the liberal men in the audience say: 'What a weird thing for a women to say to a man. Wouldn't fancy her chances.' 'Absolute cheek,' said a second. 'That's what self-assertiveness has done for them. Personally I wouldn't stand for it at all. I'd make damn sure they didn't say it twice.' The third man, older than the other two, said quietly but firmly: 'Women who make remarks like that need thoroughly putting down in my opinion.'

Unfortunately, others shared his opinion. Most of the men in the audience agreed vehemently with these remarks. Some phrased their distaste with more subtlety than others, but they seemed to agree that self-assertiveness was pushy and insolent, and was less a statement of women's needs than a deflation of men's egos.

Between the first incident in the restaurant and this incident in the concert hall we had spent much of our time urging women to change their subservient behaviour and to become more self-interested, self-assertive and to flatter men less. Suddenly, we felt that self-assertiveness may not be enough and certainly was not enough if, ultimately, it only comes down to sporadic or even systematic rudeness to chauvinistic waiters.

Assertiveness training, based on the premise that women are not skilled in stating their needs or in making their presence felt (especially when it would serve their interests best to do so), is more often associated with the genre of feminism which has developed particularly in the United States but which more recently has started to make a considerable impact in Australia, Canada, and the United Kingdom.

The idea that women should learn to act as if they believed in themselves as people with independent interests, desires and rights has been explored through a wide variety of skill-sharing workshops aimed interestingly enough not merely at older women who, we might suppose, due to years of 'faulty' socialisation, have much to learn in this direction (and we speak as two of that still stumbling, still struggling breed), but at young women, to ensure that they begin to kick the need for approval, particularly male approval, before that need becomes a lifetime's addiction. Indeed, as we write this, the current Training Calendar of the British National Association of Youth Clubs, which offers as its leading event for spring and summer 1986 'Being Assertive: A Workshop for Women', drops through the postbox. In this typically broadbased training arena, discussions, role play and practical exercises will be used to help women who want to identify and explore situations similar to those we have drawn attention to throughout this book, which cause stress, embarrassment, frustration and deep suffering to women both in their personal and professional lives. Workshops such as these, which are in themselves offshoots of successful books on related themes, are based on the underlying idea that women are so self-sacrificing that they risk becoming submerged, that they fail to develop because they fail openly to identify their aspirations, demands or necessary dues. Self-assertion courses attempt to show women that without being aggressive, manipulative or devious, they can state their exigent needs with plain speaking and straightforward action. The commonsense notion about assertion has been to assume that if women begin to promote themselves with confidence, to make known their needs, then their wishes will be granted and, to a large measure, the problem will be solved.

Before we discuss the extent to which this argument holds good and examine its defects or weaknesses, we should mention at least one strongly self-assertive woman whom we interviewed. For not *all* women reflect men. Rosie does not.

Rosie is a thirty-five-year-old American, popular college lecturer, the mother of a chubby two-year-old called May. She is deeply attached to May's father, Christopher, with whom she has had a nine-year relationship in which they agree that Christopher does a great deal of the nurturing while Rosie does ridiculously little.

This is strange. Anyone meeting Rosie would instantly remark on her gentle, caring manner, her way of building you up and her almost psychic sensitivity which lights on your badly concealed weak points and dispels them with a few comforting, practical remarks. After ten minutes conversation with Rosie one feels cosseted, protected and, somehow, rather important. People say that Christopher must be very lucky and Christopher admits his good fortune. What is unusual is that Christopher seems to be rarely reflected in this manner.

Getting to know Rosie a little better, one discovers that she has principles like iron rivets and a mind like jagged razor blades. 'Don't let her mild, melting manner fool you,' a friend said affectionately. 'Beneath the warmth she's like an intellectual steel mill.'

'I won't be ground down any more by the men I live with,' Rosie told us firmly. 'If I had to do more for my lover than he was prepared to do for me, it would be irreconcilable with my politics. So I don't.'

It is not that Rosie despises the process of reflection. Far from it: 'I think a behaviour pattern which makes as a priority not making people look small in public, not humiliating people, not embarrassing people, allowing others to keep their dignity, making them feel wanted and proud of themselves is deeply important,' she said. 'I see reflection as part of a human compassion which must be preserved. The trouble is that, firstly, women have that compassion more than men and, secondly, they use it almost solely on men and for the benefit of men.'

Rosie should know. In her first marriage, she was not the strongminded woman she is today but a soft girl overbrimming with tenderness which she used up on making her husband feel bigger and better.

'Of course he never did anything like that for me. I had very little confidence in myself in those days. Felt I was smaller, inferior to almost everyone. I was easily put down. My husband had no trouble at all reducing me to some wretched inferior servant. I complained a little. Then he ran off with my best friend, leaving me feeling I hadn't treated him well enough. I lived alone for a long time. I learnt to survive. I learnt to wean myself off reflecting men. My confidence shot up. I became truly tough within myself.

'Having learnt that I can live without a man, I choose to live with Chris because he has never demanded that I bolster him up. He has always encouraged, protected and helped me professionally and personally in ways that women traditionally help men.

'I have written extensively only since I met him, because he tells me consistently, "You're good. You can do it." If I am feeling low he says, "Are you having any problems? Try talking them through with me. I know *you* can work it out, but perhaps there is a way I can help." Chris believes in my talents, appreciates any gestures I make towards him and our home and shares everything.'

We asked Rosie to explain on what grounds their relationship stood or fell. 'That I never boost his ego. But he is quite at liberty to boost mine!' She smiled. Then on a more serious note she said: 'I demand my own space. I get it. I demand freedom to have relationships with women. I get it. I demand time to do my own work, see my own friends, keep firm links with my family and retain independent interests. I get all of it. Most of all I demand an equal share of labour in the home and the right to be treated as a full and, occasionally, as a wonderful human being!' She laughed and we gathered that she succeeded here, too.

She told us that some less fortunate couples perceive her as being selfish and Christopher as being over-generous. 'I see considering oneself as a necessary stage for women. We can't afford to relax over these key points.'

How does Christopher see the non-conforming woman in his life? He described her to us as loyal, affectionate, scrupulously fair but cautious.

'Cautious! Of course I'm cautious,' Rosie exploded, 'I'm a woman and a feminist trying to live reasonably with a man. That's enough to make anyone cautious. I've had one lousy marriage and several hellish relationships, who wouldn't be cautious?'

When their baby was due, Rosie admits that she plummeted from caution to terror. 'I became very frightened. With every couple we knew, the crunch came over child care. If the bloke did without ego-boosting before the birth, he certainly wouldn't put up with it afterwards. Nor would he assume that child rearing was half his responsibility. So even though we had seven years of reciprocal support, when May came along I knew I must be even more vigilant. I must not give an inch. It had to be a fifty/fifty division of labour over the baby. It's an issue I will not budge on. It is sacrosanct.'

How did Rosie deal with the newest and hardest problem in their domestic lives?

'I got maternity leave but I insisted that Chris took paternity leave. He had to fight to get it. That meant we could have one day on, one day off, looking after May. When I was on duty, I was on the whole time like most mothers. And I expected nothing less from him. When he was on duty I didn't want to be interrupted, asked where things were or have any jobs left over for me to do. We decided we had to eradicate any possibility of this happening by me going to a rented study on my day off and becoming inaccessible. It wasn't that easy but it worked out. And we have continued to share the upbringing of May by Chris working three-quarter time when I returned to full-time work, and both of us paying for any extra help we need. My friends understand. Most of his don't. Or they think he is crazy. But frankly that is his problem, not mine. He had to decide whose values were important.'

Cynical though we were, we had to admit that their relationship seems to work well. For Rosie's part, it could be the triumph of hope over experience, but it is tackled as an experiment in caring and careful living in which three people's lives and self-respect are at risk.

'It is terribly tiring for both of us to carry on like that,' Rosie admitted. 'We both get laughed at. Particularly as I expect my feminist views to be argued for by Chris in public as well as adhered to in private. For them not to be would anger me immensely. I can't afford concessions or compromises. I would lose out. I can't ever afford to build Chris up if it means diminishing myself, because that would diminish our relationship. As it is we are happy. What more can one ask? He is generous to me but I refuse to be grateful. Why should I? I expect a great deal from a relationship with a man.' But no more than every man we know expects from every woman we know.

We have quoted Rosie's story in full for several reasons. Rosie's self-assertive behaviour is heartening. Within her personal context Rosie's results are optimistic. But this is only half of the story. 'My forceful determination not to reflect men works domestically but becomes woefully exposed as mere bravado in the job situation,' she admitted. 'Many of the things I refuse to do for Chris, I find myself constrained to do for Tom, the liberal head of department at my college.

'Tom is my oldest colleague. We started together fifteen years ago. When we began work, we were equals and friends. He was always more insecure than I was. I gave him my support readily and tried to boost his confidence. Academic institutions are hard, competitive arenas to work in and protectiveness and solidarity, although unusual, are greatly needed. In the early days it was more of a reciprocal process. Then Tom got promoted. As a principal lecturer he has a great deal of power. Yet in some ways he is still fundamentally unsure of himself. Like many men, he is very conscious of his own dignity, very sensitive about being shown up or being humiliated, and he relies on me for support. I protect him a lot. Why? I protect him a little bit for old times' sake, for the warmth and friendship we once had, but more I protect him because he has power over me.

'It is important for my own job security that I do not irritate him. Therefore although I take him on directly in terms of battles over students' needs and treatment, or how courses should be taught, it seems politic and useful not to take him on over day-to-day things that matter to his ego. For instance, when there is a staff meeting and someone suggests that a change is made in one of Tom's courses, I choose not to take him on then and not to give that other member of staff justified support. Tom would become defensive, take it as a personal criticism and he would make a feeble attempt to retain his course. I would know the argument was flaky, I know I could tear it to shreds, but I don't. What I do is very unassertive and very indirect. I put a lot of hard work and time in trying to deal with the problem in a roundabout way so that he doesn't feel shown up or threatened. I spend hours working out alternative structures to that course, then I try and persuade him that it's his idea and that it's a good one. I put in all the work he should have put in, simply to protect him. Of course Tom isn't grateful. He feels my behaviour is his due.'

As we saw in Chapter Eight, most of the women we interviewed reflected men because they were unable to avoid the varying sanctions that were imposed if they refused to do so. Rosie was unusual in that at least in her social and personal life she managed to stand up for herself, speak up for other women and survive. However, even her self-assertive attitudes became toned down, moderated and marginalised outside the home. Indeed she fell into the kind of deceit and manipulation which Anne Dickson, author of the best selling *A Woman in Your Own Right: Assertiveness and You* (1982), attempts to steer women away from.

The story of Rosie, the woman who cannot afford to compromise at home but cannot afford *not* to compromise at work, pinpoints one of the problems in the self-assertiveness philosophy in terms of its usefulness in resisting the impulse to reflect men.

Assertiveness training is supposed to help women who lack control over their own lives. But many women have no control over vast areas of their lives. Rosie is luckier than many but her situation highlights certain deficiencies in the self-assertiveness theory. Even the National Association of Youth Clubs, having outlined the advantages of self-assertion in their Training Calendar are forced to admit that, 'Assertion is not aggression nor is it necessarily getting what you want, but it can lead to more open honest and rewarding communication with others at home and at work.' Even Anne Dickson is obliged to recognise that although the newly confident woman has acknowledged 'that she is in charge of her actions, her choices and her life' (p.8), 'choosing to behave assertively may mean not getting exactly what you want but having to negotiate a compromise instead' (p.13). For although the assertive woman persistently states her right to be treated as an equal human being, and Anne Dickson stresses that 'this principle of equality is one of the most important hallmarks of assertive behaviour' (p.13), when women are faced with someone 'who for one reason or another has more power or a higher status than we do, it can be difficult to assert our rights as an equal' (p.12). Anne Dickson rightly states that 'given our prevailing culture, women are, with obvious exceptions, in less powerful positions than men' (p.xii). Although she acknowledges that this crucial point 'can be made into an overtly political issue' (p.xii), this is not the purpose of her book and she fails to explore the issue.

Assertiveness-training procedures are undoubtedly effective in helping some women to live more powerfully. When women like Rosie use these confidence-boosting tools to stop reflecting individual men, they are often rewarded with personal success and achieve a measure of control over their domestic lives. However, this remains essentially an individual solution to a widespread problem; if assertiveness training is considered in relation to the social phenomenon of male reflection, confidence-improving techniques have neither affected nor altered the over-all status of women in our society to date.

There are two major flaws in the assumption that if women start to assert themselves the problem of male reflection will be solved. Firstly, it puts the pressure on women to change when, as we have seen, it is precisely women who do not have the power (economic, sexual or political) to change their environment.

It is extremely difficult for women to stand up for their rights. As we pointed out in the early chapters, social conditioning at home, and educational processes later, conspire to thwart women's power and self-esteem. And, as we saw in Chapter Eight, assertive women are typically subject to abusive treatment. It is no solution to tell a women who is being systematically beaten to stand up for herself and demand her dues; this may well be how she came to be battered in the first place. Above all, as we saw in Chapter Six, many women are financially dependent on men. It does not serve their interests to demand caring treatment from an uncaring provider. When men have financial and physical power and are prepared to use it, no advice to women about the kind of nurturing they need is necessarily going to work.

Where self-assertion does work, however, is in terms of women's self-respect and self-esteem. Confidence in ourselves, a full sense of our own worth, enables us to see that our needs are as important as those of our husbands, our boyfriends, our fathers. In the same way that the slogans 'black is beautiful' and 'glad to be gay' aimed to cultivate dignity, so the slogan 'sisterhood is powerful' aimed to invest women with the inner strength necessary to continue to struggle for liberation. However, all three slogans were less about asserting rights than about establishing values.

" HELLO, DARLING. WE'RE CONDUCTING A POLL ON SEXUAL HARASSMENT. "

This brings us to the second flaw in the self-assertiveness strategy: it urges women to be more like men. But the evidence gathered throughout this book makes it clear that it is not women's behaviour which is wrong; rather, it is the fact that this behaviour is not reciprocated. Reflective behaviour is congenial, useful and productive. It is a method of achieving harmony. It is

185

the key to making people believe they can stretch themselves beyond their most daring dreams. There is nothing wrong with considering others, putting them at their ease, managing their emotions to make them feel good, expanding their confidence, extending their abilities, improving their performance or nurturing their spirit. *What is wrong is that women do it for men and men do not do it for women.*

In our view, there should be more rather than less of this behaviour. It is the asymmetry which is at fault: an asymmetry which profits men at the expense of women. Who looks after women? Who helps women to expand? Who gives wives, girlfriends, mothers, daughters and sisters the self-confidence and protection that is their due?

For women to become self-assertive may be a necessary defence in the patriarchal society within which women struggle to survive but it is not the whole answer. Assertiveness training is not enough. Men have to start to be accommodating. Men have to learn to provide emotional support.

It would actually be wasteful for women to throw away their nurturing skills when, at their best, these are compassionate and fruitful actions. As Virginia Woolf (1928) pointed out, reflecting the figure of man is a 'delicious power' (p.35) and without that power the earth would probably still be made up of swamp and jungle. Whatever their use in civilised societies, mirrors are essential to heroic as well as to violent action. Sadly we live in a world of heroes. Heroines have scant space and less recognition within its boundaries. Adding to Virginia Woolf's contention that 'the looking-glass vision is of supreme importance because it charges the vitality' (p.36), we would suggest that as our society, no less than hers, needs all the healthy vitality it can accrue, both sexes need this charge. For years women have reflected men and this human behaviour has been constantly used against them. The same behaviour could, and should, be used in women's interests . . . but that is another book.

BIBLIOGRAPHY

ADLER, Larry, 1984
It Ain't Necessarily So
Collins, London
ATWOOD, Margaret, 1983
Second Words
House of Arian's Press
BEEZLEY MRAZEK, P., M. LYNCH and A. BENTOVIM, 1981
'Sexual Abuse of Children in the United Kingdom', unpub-
lished MS. cited in Jalna Hanmer, 'Violence Against Women',
The Changing Experience of Woman, Unit 15, Open University
Press, 1983
BELOTTI, Elena Gianini, 1975
Little Girls
Writers' and Readers', London
BENGIS, Ingrid, 1974
Combat in the Erogenous Zone
Quartet Books, London
BISHOP, Beata, with Pat MCNEILL, 1977
Below the Belt: An Irreverent Analysis of the Male Ego
Coventure, London
BUTLER, Sandra, 1979
The Conspiracy of Silence
Bantam Books, New York
BYRNE, Eileen, 1978
Women and Education
Tavistock, London
CASSELL, Joan, 1977
A Group Called Women
David McKay, New York
CHERNIN, Kim, 1981
Womansize: The Tyranny of Slenderness
The Women's Press, London
CHESLER, Phyllis, 1978
About Men

The Women's Press, London

CHESLER, Phyllis and Emily Jane GOODMAN, 1976
Women, Money and Power
William Marrow, New York

CLARRICOATES, Katherine, 1978
' "Dinosaurs in the Classroom": A re-examination of some aspects of the "hidden" curriculum in primary schools' in *Women's Studies International Quarterly*, Vol I, no 2, pp165–174

COOPER, Jilly, 1969
How to Stay Married
Methuen, London

COWARD, Rosalind, 1984
Female Desire: Women's Sexuality Today
Paladin, London

DARIAUX, Geneviève Antoine, 1967
The Men in Your Life
F. Muller, London

DEPARTMENT OF EDUCATION AND SCIENCE, 1975
Curriculum for Boys and Girls
Education Survey 21, HMSO, London

DICKSON, Anne, 1982
A Woman in Your Own Right: Assertiveness and You
Quartet, London

DOBASH, Rebecca Emerson and Russell DOBASH, 1979
Violence Against Wives: A Case Against the Patriarchy
Macmillan, New York

DWORKIN, Andrea, 1983
Right-Wing Women: The Politics of Domesticated Females
The Women's Press, London

EASLEA, Brian, 1980
Witch-hunting, Magic and the New Philosophy: An Introduction to the Debates of the Scientific Revolution 1450–1750
Harvester Press, Brighton

EHRENREICH, Barbara, 1983
The Hearts of Men: American Dreams and the Flight from Commitment
Pluto Press, London

EQUAL OPPORTUNITIES COMMISSION, 1983
The Fact About Women Is . . .
E.O.C., Manchester

FARLEY, Lin, 1978
Sexual Shakedown: the Sexual Harassment of Women on the Job
McGraw Hill, New York

FENNEMA, Elizabeth, 1980

'Success in Maths' paper presented at conference,
Sex Differentiation in Schooling
Churchill College, Cambridge, January 2–5

FINKELHOR, David, 1979
Sexually Victimized Children
Free Press, New York

FIRESTONE, Shulamith, (1970) 1979
The Dialectic of Sex
The Women's Press, London

FRIEDAN, Betty, 1963
The Feminine Mystique
Penguin, Harmondsworth

FRIEDAN, Betty, 1982
The Second Stage
Michael Joseph, London

FRIEZE, Irene Hanson, 1983
'Investigating the Causes and Consequences of Marital Rape'
in *Signs* Vol VIII, no 3, pp532–553

GOFFMAN, Erving, 1963
Behaviour in Public Places: Notes on the Social Organization of Gatherings
Free Press, New York

GREER, Germaine, 1970
The Female Eunuch
MacGibbon & Kee, London

GREER, Germaine, 1984
Sex and Destiny
Secker & Warburg, London

HAMILTON, Cicely, 1909
Marriage as a Trade
Reprinted 1981, The Women's Press, London

HANMER, Jalna, (ed), 1983
Violence Against Women
The Changing Experience of Women: Unit 15,
Open University Press

HANMER, Jalna and Sheila SAUNDERS, 1984
Well Founded Fear
Hutchinson, London

HENLEY, Nancy, 1977
Body Politics
Power Sex and Non-Verbal Communication
Prentice Hall, New Jersey

HERMAN, Judith Lewis, 1981
Father–Daughter Incest

Harvard University Press,
Cambridge, Massachusetts
HITE, Shere, 1976
The Hite Report
Dell Publishing, New York
HOCHSCHILD, Arlie, 1984
The Managed Heart
University of California Press, California
HORNER, Matina, 1976
'Toward an Understanding of Achievement-related Conflict in Women' in
Judith Stacey *et al* (eds)
And Jill Came Tumbling After
Dell, New York, pp43-63
HOWE, Florence, 1976
'The Education of Women' in
Judith Stacey *et al* (eds) *And Jill Came Tumbling After*,
Dell Publishing, New York pp64–78
INGHAM, Mary, 1984
Men
Century, London
KEMPTON, Sally, 1978
'Cutting Loose' in
Elaine Partnow (ed) *The Quotable Woman*
Anchor Books, Doubleday, New York
MACKENZIE, Midge, 1975
Shoulder to Shoulder
Penguin, Harmondsworth
MACKINNON, Catherine, 1979
Sexual Harassment of Working Women
Yale University Press, New Haven and London
MCROBBIE, Angela, 1978
'Working Class Girls and the Culture of Femininity' in
Women's Studies Group (eds),
Women Take Issue: Aspects of Women's Surbordination
Hutchinson, London
MARTIN, Susan E., 1981
'Sexual Harassment in the Workplace: from Occupational Hazard to Sexual Discrimination'
Paper delivered, *Law and Society* Annual Meeting
Amherst, Massachusetts
MASTERS, William and Virginia JOHNSON, 1966
Human Sexual Responses
Little, Brown, Boston

MILLER, Jean Baker, 1976
  Toward A New Psychology of Women
  Penguin, Harmondsworth
MORGAN, Marabel, 1973
  The Total Woman
  Hodder & Stoughton, London
MORGAN, Robin, 1970
  'Letter to a Sister Underground' in
  Robin Morgan (ed)
  Sisterhood is Powerful
  Vintage Books, New York
NEWSOM, John, 1948
  The Education of Girls
  Faber, London
OAKLEY, Ann, 1974
  The Sociology of Housework
  Martin Robertson, Oxford
OAKLEY, Ann, 1980
  Women Confined: Toward a Sociology of Childbirth
  Martin Robertson, Oxford
OAKLEY, Ann, 1981
  Subject Woman
  Martin Robertson, Oxford
OLSEN, Tillie, 1980
  Silences: When Writers Don't Write
  Virago, London
ORBACH, Susie, 1978
  Fat is a Feminist Issue
  Hamlyn Paperbacks, Middlesex
PARLIAMENTARY SELECT COMMITTEE on
  Violence in Marriage, 1975
  Report from the Select Committee on Violence in Marriage
  Together with the Proceedings of the Committee
  Vol II, Session 1974/5
  HMSO London
PARTNOW, Elaine (ed), 1978
  The Quotable Woman
  Anchor Books, Doubleday, New York
PEARCE, Diana and Hariette MCADOO, 1981
  Women and Children: Alone and in Poverty
  Center for National Poverty Review, Washington D.C.
RHODES, Dusty and Sandra MCNEILL, 1985
  Women Against Violence Against Women
  Onlywomen Press, London

RICH, Adrienne, 1979
   On Lies, Secrets and Silence
   Reprinted 1980, Virago, London
RICH, Adrienne, 1981
   Compulsory Heterosexuality and Lesbian Existence
   Onlywomen Press, London
RUSSELL, Diane, 1976
   The Politics of Rape
   Stein & Day, New York
RUSSELL, Diana E. H., 1982
   Rape in Marriage
   MacMillan, New York
SCOTT, Hilda, 1984
   Working Your Way to the Bottom: The Feminization of Poverty
   Pandora Press, London
SCOTT, Marion, 1980
   'Teach Her a Lesson' in
   Dale Spender and Elizabeth Sarah, (eds) *Learning to Lose*
   The Women's Press, London
SMAIL, Barbara, 1985
   Girl-Friendly Science: Avoiding Sex Bias in the Classroom
   School Curriculum Development Committee Report
SPENDER, Dale, 1980
   Man Made Language
   Routledge & Kegan Paul, London, 2nd ed. 1985
SPENDER, Dale, 1984
   'Sexism in Teacher Education' in
   Sandra Acker and David Warren Piper (eds) *Is Higher Education Fair to Women?*
   SRHE & NFER, Nelson, Surrey pp132-142
STACEY, Judith, 1983
   'The New Conservative Feminism'
   Feminist Studies, Vol 9, No 3, pp559–584
STANHO, Elizabeth A., 1985
   Intimate Intrusions: Women's Experience of Male Violence
   Routledge & Kegan Paul, London
STANTON, Elizabeth Cady, *et al*, 1881
   History of Woman Suffrage
   Fowler and Wells, New York reprinted 1969 Arno/*The New York Times*, New York
STEINEM, Gloria, 1984
   Outrageous Acts and Everyday Rebellions
   Jonathan Cape, London
STRACHEY, Ray, 1928

The Cause: A Short History of the Women's Movement in Great Britain
G. Bell & Sons, London; reprinted 1979, Virago, London
TOBIAS, Sheila, 1978
Overcoming Math Anxiety
Norton, New York
WALDEN, Rosie and Valerie WALKERDINE, 1985
Girls and Mathematics: From Primary to Secondary Schooling
Bedford Way Papers: 24
University of London Institute of Education
WARD, Elizabeth, 1984
Father–Daughter Rape
The Women's Press, London
WEST, Rebecca, 1982
The Young Rebecca: Writings of Rebecca West, 1911–1917
Jane Marcus (ed)
Virago, London
WHARTON, Edith, 1900
'The Touchstone'
Scribner's Magazine, XXVII (January–July)
WHYTE, Judith, Rosemary DEEM, Lesley KANT and Maureen CRUICKSHANK, (eds) 1985
Girl Friendly Schooling
Methuen/London
WOLLSTONECRAFT, Mary, 1792
Vindication of the Rights of Woman
Johnson, London
WOOLF, Virginia, 1928
A Room of One's Own
reprinted 1974, Penguin, Harmondsworth